The 30-Minute Stock Trader

The 30-MINUTE STOCK TRADER

The Stress-Free Trading Strategy
for Financial Freedom

LAURENS BENSDORP

THE 30-MINUTE STOCK TRADER
The Stress-Free Trading Strategy for Financial Freedom

ISBN   978-1-61961-550-2   *Paperback*
       978-1-61961-573-1   *Hardcover*
       978-1-61961-551-9   *Ebook*

INTERIOR DESIGN BY
Kevin Barrett Kane

LIONCREST
PUBLISHING

To my dear children,
Jose, Naty, and Sofia

Acknowledgments

This book would not be possible without my parents. Because you allowed me to trade your money back in 2000, I acquired the confidence to step into the trading world, which brought me here. Now that I'm a parent myself, I know how hard (and rewarding) parenting can be, and my admiration and gratitude has multiplied. Thank you for always supporting me. I love you deeply.

My dear wife, Madelin, understands me better than anyone, and she has provided me great help and motivation in writing this book. Your love and inner and outer beauty is a privilege I'm grateful to enjoy daily. Your compassion and understanding in helping me achieve my mission in life is endless. I love you.

A special thanks to Tom Basso for taking the time to write the foreword. Every time we talk, time seems to fly, and I pick up such wise lessons that I take to heart. His approach to trading combined with the choice to have the best life possible is what taught me to design the life and trading style that suits me best. Thank you, Tom.

To my Elite Mentoring students: You are a wonderful group

of people—teaching you brings me incredible joy. You are the drive that keeps me working on new strategies and improving myself. Your bright minds and questions keep me sharp, and you have taught me more than you will ever know.

Disclaimer

It should not be assumed that the methods, techniques, or indicators presented in these products will be profitable or will not result in losses. Past results are not necessarily indicative of future results. Examples presented in this book are for educational purposes only. These trading setups are not solicitations of any orders to buy or sell. The author, the publisher, and all affiliates assume no responsibility for your trading results. There is a high degree of risk in trading.

Hypothetical or simulated performance results have certain inherent limitations. Unlike an actual performance record, simulated results do not represent actual trading. Also, since the trades have not actually been executed, the results may have under- or overcompensated for the impact, if any, of certain market factors, such as lack of liquidity. Simulated trading programs in general are also subject to the fact that they are designed with the benefit of hindsight. No representation is being made that any account will or is likely to achieve profits or losses similar to those shown.

Why I Wrote This Book

Understandably, a lot of people ask: If you're so good at trading, why do you teach? Why don't you just trade your own money? In this book, I reveal profitable trading strategies. Why would I do that for less than twenty bucks? It's a fair question, so I'd like to give my honest answer.

I started trading back in 2000, and I spent thousands of dollars and hours searching for the Holy Grail of trading strategies. Despite devouring all of the information I could get my hands on, I wound up learning what to do based on trial and error. There just wasn't a lot of good information out there. I wished someone cared enough to show me a strategy with a clear edge, holding my hand as I learned the ropes. Nobody like that existed.

I know how hard it is to learn how to trade. No matter how smart you are or how hard you try, it can feel like years of helplessly swimming in the deep end.

The truth is, successful trading can be simple, but we humans have a tendency to think we need to complicate things in order to get outstanding results. As I'll explain in the book, winning trading isn't about finding the perfect strategy—it's about knowing yourself so that you can identify the perfect strategy for *you*. Everyone is different and must know his or her strengths, weaknesses, personality, risk tolerance, and personal situation. Trading is far more boring and process-oriented than people like to think.

One of the best ways to master a skill is to teach it. This is common advice, but it's something I've noticed in my own life many times over. While teaching my Elite Mentoring students, I'm forced to dig into my strategies deeper and deeper so that I can explain every part clearly. Teaching keeps me honest and hungry. Since beginning to teach, my trading knowledge has multiplied exponentially, and I've eliminated many of my strategies' flaws and weaknesses. My students are some of the smartest traders I know, and interacting with them sharpens my mind daily.

It's the perfect combination: I get enjoyment out of teaching a group of focused, successful, like-minded people, and we both improve our trading skills.

My mission in life is to help others transform themselves, because as I'll explain in the book, it took a lot of self-work for me to become the trader and person I am today. Trading is a lonely profession, and my process-oriented approach can be as boring as it is successful. Teaching is the opposite—it gives me joy, while sharpening my skills. I love to help others, and I love to develop new strategies and ideas and challenge my past beliefs.

When I was younger, I taught white-water rafting guides how to improve their performance and skills. I quickly found that I was good at helping others, and that I loved it. I later discovered my passion and skill for strategic trading. Then it was obvious that my mission in life was to combine the two. My calling is to help others make money by creating their own strategic trading approaches.

Every strategy in this book has a clear edge, is simple in nature, and is easy to follow. They are not the only strategies that work. They are frameworks—the start of what your eventual strategies will look like, depending on your beliefs, objectives, personality, and risk tolerance. The strategies can be tweaked in multiple ways, to best suit *you*. Everybody is different and thus should have a different trading methodology.

As long as you follow the steps outlined in this book, and have evidence that your personal approach actually works, you will succeed. Whether you do this on your own, or through my teaching, I achieve my mission. I want you to succeed. When you succeed, I'm happy and fulfilled. Good luck, and thank you for reading.

For more information and exclusive offers, please visit *tradingmasteryschool.com*.

All graphics contained in this book are also available at *tradingmasteryschool.com/charts-30-minute-stock-trader*.

Kind Regards,
Laurens Bensdorp

Table of Contents

Foreword / XVII

PART 1: HOW AUTOMATED TRADING CAN SET YOU FREE

1 *Smells Like Financial Freedom* / 3

2 *The Thirty-Minute Trader* / 17

PART 2: BEATING THE "EXPERTS"

3 *The "Experts" Are Stealing Your Money* / 43

4 *Proof Automated Trading Works* / 50

PART 3: BUILDING YOUR PERFECT THIRTY-MINUTE TRADING STATEGY

5 *What It Takes—First, Know Thyself* / 59

6 *The Beliefs All Top Traders Share* / 67

7 *The Secret Twelve-Ingredient Recipe* / 89

PART 4: MEET THE PROVEN STRATEGIES

8 Weekly Rotation S&P 500—For the Busy or Lazy / 103

9 Mean-Reversion Long—For Bold Contrarians / 119

10 Mean-Reversion Short—Make Money in Bad Markets / 137

PART 5: THE EXPONENTIAL MAGIC OF COMBINING STRATEGIES

11 Weekly Rotation + Mean-Reversion Short—Trend Following without Big Drawdowns / 153

12 Mean-Reversion Long and Short Combined—Lower Risk, Higher Upside / 160

PART 6: CONCLUSION—THE FINAL STEPS TO FINANCIAL FREEDOM

13 *The Missing Ingredient—Position-Sizing (To Achieve Your Objectives)* / 169

14 *Turn It Loose—But Watch Out for This Pitfall* / 174

15 *The Next Step* / 187

About the Author / 191

Foreword

BY TOM BASSO

I started investing when I had some extra money from delivering newspapers at twelve years old and bought a mutual fund with that money. Some fifty-two years later, I'm still investing. It's been a long and very rewarding ride through investing in mutual funds, then stocks, then futures, then starting a Registered Investment Advisor company, registering as a Commodity Trading Advisor in the United States, trading FOREX, retiring, and now managing my retirement portfolios. I still have a love of the process. I enjoy learning new concepts and inventing different approaches to the process of good investing.

I first met Laurens a number of years ago after he had made some contact with Van Tharp, the trading coach, and he had read *The New Market Wizards* and a few of my other interviews with industry-based authors. He knew a lot more about me than I did about him when he contacted me. That changed when he visited my summer home in the Arizona mountains, and we had some lengthy discussions about business, investing, and life. Laurens impressed me as a "man of the world" due to his speaking several languages, having business interests and experience in many parts of the globe, and having a great deal of experience, good and bad, with the investment process. I have since met him in Hong Kong, and I periodically have Skype chats with him.

I was very interested in seeing what Laurens pulled together in this book because he has so many experiences that I never have had. I dug in and read it in about two days off and on, anytime I had a moment to continue reading. I could not put it down!

In Part 2, where Laurens discusses automated trading, you get a great summary of some of the great benefits that can come from using the computer to shore up some of your potential weaknesses in execution. The computer becomes a mindless slave. When you program a logical approach to trading into the machine, it obeys and executes according to that logic. There will be no exceptions as long as you keep the program running successfully and feed the machine electricity.

Part 3 of the book has some excellent points concerning self-examination and beliefs. I've known people that believe "money is evil," others that are greedy with no objective goal other than greed, and others who don't want to spend even a minute on managing their net worth. If you are not prepared to examine yourself and your beliefs, you will surely fail at whatever investment approach you try. You will find a way to sabotage it sooner or later. His list of beliefs that all top traders share is an excellent read and probably a part of the book traders should copy and put in front of themselves to reread often.

In Part 3, he absolutely nails the concept of investing a great deal of effort in your own personal investment approach. Because of my notoriety, I get lots of questions from new traders asking, "What do you use for your buy/sell approach?" I tell them over and over that I am not the same person they are. I have different knowledge, skills, capital to allocate, and experience with trading. It doesn't make any sense to me that anyone would want to trade exactly as I trade. I try to help them understand that they need to develop a trading strategy that will work for them and not try to copy me.

The next idea that Laurens talks about in Part 3 is the systematizing of the investment strategy. I remember one year when I sorted all the trades I made in a calendar year from highest profit to largest loss and noticed that one trade in Japanese Yen that I had held all year long was the difference between making a large single-digit gain that year and breaking even. In other words, had I overridden or missed that single Yen trade, all the other good work I did all year long would have been worth nothing. The next year I performed the same exercise and found that two trades were the difference between a double-digit gain and breaking even. That surely emphasized to me the need to execute my strategies as close to perfection as is humanly possible.

This example shows how important it is to follow your rules in a trend-following trading strategy. However, that is not the only way to trade. Some might opt for a mean-reversion strategy such as those outlined in Laurens's book. You will still need to execute your trades as perfectly as possible, but there will be less dependence on one to two trades per year. It all comes down to what fits you the best.

Being human means having flaws, making mistakes from time to time, and possibly not being able to execute a trading strategy flawlessly. Enter the computer. Since I am a chemical engineer by degree, I found it straightforward to program the various steps I was taking into a series of programs that essentially did my trading strategy for me. I spent years working hard to put myself out of work. No longer did I have to concern myself with being on a vacation or being sick. My automated trading strategies executed the orders that should be executed without flaw.

I didn't have to concern myself with what was happening in the world, either. When George Soros had his famous billion-dollar short profit on the British Pound, I was short the Pound as well. My profits were not at all due to my investment brilliance or thinking. They were simply because the British Pound had gone into a down trend, my computerized strategy yielded a sell signal and went short, and I profited from that action. It was the same exact decision-making that would lead to the next one thousand trades that my strategy would execute. Guessing what someone like Soros or any other "famous" money manager is going to do or agonizing over volumes of fundamental data to make a decision will just make you exhausted, confused, and unable to pull the trigger on many trades. That would definitely not help your cause much. Laurens points this out in his book multiple times, and he's dead on with that advice, in my opinion. To Laurens and me, trading is a numbers game. The larger the amount of sample size in number of trades, the more we hope to create probable success. In some of the strategies I traded, I knew that over two-thirds of my trades would be losses, but I also knew that when I was with the market, I would have trades that had sizable profits to make up for the smaller losing trades. Replicating that process over and over in a tireless fashion got me to where I wanted to be, instead of just being lucky every now and then with one spectacular winning trade.

Laurens captures perfectly in Part 4 the importance of understanding who you are and designing your approach to the markets in a way that will make you successful in trading. This single concept is probably the most frequent reason that traders fail. They may have a decent strategy and decent risk control, but they interject their own fears and emotions into the trading, causing the strategy not to be executed correctly, resulting in the strategy's downfall. At that point, they're off to the next great idea, and the process is repeated to major frustration. With some easy-to-understand examples, he shows how various personalities match up to very different approaches to trading and how all of them can work going forward. I'm more of a trend follower at heart, but that is not how all traders should trade. There are a lot of pathways to success in trading, and you have to find yours.

Another aspect that Laurens gets right in Part 5 is the concept that if you can automate your decision-making process to a large extent, you are not limited to one fixed strategy. When I ran Trendstat Capital Management with $600 million under management back in the day, we were trading stocks, 20+ mutual funds, 70+ futures markets, 30+ foreign exchange pairs, and 10 commodity options using multiple strategies within each investment area. Daily execution was handled by only two traders with a team of four computer experts, including myself, and three people in administration backing them up. And talk about scalable—we could have handled twice as much with the same people simply by adding a few inexpensive computer servers! Laurens shows some simple examples of how combining together strategies logically should increase the robustness of your overall trading, increase reliability, increase return to risk measures, and help you achieve more long-term success in trading. I have not used some of the specific software that Laurens talks about in the book, but I have little doubt that Laurens and his programmer have done their finest in marrying the concepts outlined in the book to the software and getting it to function smoothly. The investing process at that point becomes routine, almost boring. We all unemotionally brush our teeth daily and think nothing of it even though it leads to good dental health in the long term. Running your investment strategy can be just as routine and unemotional, leading you to long-term financial health.

Chapter 14 in Part 6 covers some important forward-looking advice to would-be traders. Your strategy, no matter how well suited for you and well researched it is, will still have to react to new things that the market will throw at you. How well the strategy adapts to changing conditions will dictate some of your future success. He correctly implores the reader to "treat it like a business." That is all it is. As Laurens points out, if you want excitement, thrills, and adrenaline fixes, find them elsewhere. If you trade to satisfy those needs, the markets will shred you.

That doesn't mean you don't have other challenges as a trader. Even with systemized strategies, you will have issues with executing brokers, financial crises that create aberrant trading challenges, power and internet outages that can be trying, and countless times when you don't feel like doing anything with your trading. But I promise you, if you can take the business approach to the process of investing that Laurens's book maps out, you have a shot at getting out of your own way, and you, too, can "enjoy the ride" of successful investing.

– Tom Basso

Featured in *The New Market Wizards* as "Mr. Serenity" by Jack Schwager

Author *of Panic-Proof Investing: Lessons in Profitable Investing from a Market Wizard*

Former CEO of Trendstat Capital Management, Inc.

Former director of the National Futures Association, one of the US regulatory organizations

Former arbitrator for the National Futures Association

Former director of the Society of Asset Allocators and Fund Timers, Inc. (SAAFTI), now known as the National Association of Active Investment Managers (NAAIM)

Bachelor of Science in Chemical Engineering from Clarkson

University, Potsdam, NY

Master in Business Administration from Southern Illinois University at Edwardsville

Creator of a website dedicated to trader education: enjoytheride.world

Chairman of the Board of Standpoint Funds in Scottsdale, Arizona, a fund management company specializing in all weather funds combining equity and futures approaches in one portfolio.

Now happily retired and enjoying the ride!

PART 1

How Automated Trading Can Set You Free

CHAPTER 1

Smells Like Financial Freedom

You pop your head outside the window of your office, and you can hear the ocean. You're doing your thirty minutes of daily "work," entering your orders into the broker platform. You could have done it first thing in the morning, but you decided to go for a swim in the ocean instead. Afterward, you'll go cycling in the mountains, and spend uninterrupted time at night with your wife and children. Tomorrow, you'll swim for as long as you want to, again. You don't have a boss, so nobody is nagging you to get back to work.

Then, tomorrow you'll put in your thirty minutes of work and won't feel like doing anything else that day. You'll call your wife. "Want to drive two hundred miles to Seville?" You go and explore an exotic city with the love of your life on a Tuesday afternoon.

You're living a life of financial freedom, and three hundred days of sun, in southern Spain. Next week, you're off to the

Caribbean coast in South America, with your family, to visit your wife's hometown. You'll take your "work" with you: your thirty minutes a day of pressing a few buttons to maintain the financial freedom your automated trading strategy has granted you.

During the same trip, you'll visit Costa Rica, in which you have various business interests unrelated to trading, giving you additional passive income.

You do whatever *you* want, whenever *you* want. You only work when you're in the mood.

The strategy fits *your* lifestyle. You can live by the ocean in Europe and swim every day, or you can live in the American suburbs and take your kids to soccer practice. You can live life on your own terms, because you'll be making passive income while you sleep.

No more reporting to bosses, no schedule that tells you where you need to be or what you should be doing. Instead of other people deciding how you should live, your life is up to you.

If you don't want to work one day, you won't work, because you have enough passive income coming in to cover your expenses, and then some. If you want a longer conversation with your wife or kids, you'll have it. You have the maximum amount of joy and freedom possible, because every day, you create the most perfect day you can imagine.

You had to work hard, up front, of course, to build your automated trading strategy. But it has granted you lifelong financial independence, allowing you to live wherever you want and do whatever you want. You can work on passion projects, stay active, travel whenever you want, and spend uninterrupted quality time with family and friends.

That's my life right now.

I'm really not trying to brag. The truth is, my editor had to wring that description out of me, because after having freedom for so long, it seems normal to me. It's how life should be, for anyone who wants it. And there's zero reason you can't have it, too.

You'll have to want it badly enough to work hard at first. Fortunately for you, I'll lay out each step in this book, and once you're done, it will only require thirty minutes of daily maintenance.

I have students who are successful, highly paid executives, but they still have to deal with nagging bosses, annoying bureaucracy, and management telling them what to do. They have pressure, deadlines, and targets to meet. It causes a lot of stress, and they're uncomfortable.

For all of them, there comes a time when they say it's not worth the money.

Are you in the same boat?

It's your turn to create financial freedom without the obligations of a stressful job. Here are the basics.

Trade once a day—no intraday market monitoring required. You enter your trades and download the new updated historical data from your data provider, because that data will tell you what to do tomorrow. Then you open your trading software (your scanning and back-testing software), and you scan the previous day's data. Your software tells you which new positions to enter, based on the proven rules you programmed into it long ago.

In five minutes, your computer will calculate what you should do. Do you need to adjust existing orders? Close out current positions? This would take you *days* to calculate— scanning the complete universe of approximately seven thousand US-listed stocks, and generating perfect trading decisions on when to buy and sell. The computer does that in minutes, emotion-, stress-, and error-free.

You will never have to monitor your positions during the day. The only thing that monitoring can do is provoke you to override your proven strategy. The same goes for TV and news. The Fed is making an announcement? Ignore it. Ignore it all, and live your life, while the strategy makes you money.

Most traders let their lives be guided by the news—by the latest profit warning, corporate action, or Fed announcement. It causes useless stress, and it's nothing more than guessing.

Let's say I'm trading for an investor, and something like Brexit happens. Of course, it was all over the news. Everyone said it was a disaster. I read the news after coming home from dinner at 1:00 a.m. one night, and I shrugged. It was interesting, but I wasn't at all worried about my portfolio. In fact, I was excited to see what the day would bring, because my strategy was prepared.

I went into the office early to look at my positions, and I was market-neutral invested, meaning that I had both long and short positions, and was completely hedged.

For half of the day, I had to ease the concerns of unnecessarily anxious investors. I understood why they were worried, but they didn't need to be. Our automated strategies were prepared for all market conditions, even extreme ones like Brexit. They couldn't avoid the constant news message shouting fear and doom—analysts telling you exactly what would happen, based on nothing.

I had people calling me expressing concern, even though they knew nothing about my positions. Most people can't ignore the fear and noise in media.

The markets went way down for a few days, then reacted sharply the other way, and nobody talks about it anymore. It was just noise.

Whenever there is news, I get calls. It's amazing. Mostly when that happens, my mean-reversion strategies, which buy fear, work well. It doesn't matter, though, because statistical strategies and automation mean that news is irrelevant. I don't need to have any anxiety, and neither do the people you trade for.

You have clear rules on when to buy or sell, and your software tells you *exactly* what to do. You follow its instructions, because you put in the hard work beforehand to ensure you are following a proven formula to make money, long term. The agenda of the news and the whims of your emotions are completely absent.

I'll take you through, step by step, but it's simple. Trading doesn't have to be hard—as long as you follow the rules, and as long as you create a strategy that suits *your* personality, *your* lifestyle, and *your* risk tolerance. The first step is rigorous self-analysis, which I'll walk you through in the book. What are your beliefs of the markets? Do you like trend following? Mean reversion? Why? Do you want to trade both long and short, or just long? Do you want to enter orders daily, weekly, or monthly? Are you patient or impatient, and what does that mean for your potential strategy?

The clearer your objectives, the easier it is to define your exact strategy, as we'll discuss in part 3.

There are many strategies that work, but only the one you pick has to fit your unique situation. The strategies use the same fundamental principles, but their execution is different, and if they don't fit your personality, you will fail. It's not that hard to consistently beat the markets, year after year, once you've determined your ideal strategy. But if you don't take the time to analyze yourself, you'll override your strategy.

Our emotions often unconsciously get the best of us, which is why I automate everything. Automation takes emotion completely out of the equation. It's just a computer crunching numbers, and you blindly obey.

I advocate *strategic trading*, as opposed to *discretionary trading*.

Discretionary traders are trying to anticipate what the market will do, by perfectly analyzing information. The information is imperfect, though, and analyzing it perfectly takes Buffett-esque skill. It's subjective. Discretionary traders follow loose rules, which make them vulnerable to emotional swings. They need to be "right" in picking stocks, so they often take losses personally. When they're wrong, their ego is hurt. They're very "flavor of the month," using a variety of indicators based on the times. Some use macroeconomic indicators, chart patterns, or even news. It's nonquantitative, and they generally have a tiny watch list of stocks and markets to trade, because they can't possibly track the whole trading universe like computers.

Strategic traders are virtually the opposite. They aren't *anticipating* what the market is doing; they're *participating* in what the market is actually, currently doing. It's a humble, realistic approach that takes ego out of the equation. They follow prices, rather than information. They have a few rules that are strict and well defined, to govern their entries, exits, risk management, and position sizing. Because their ego is absent, they're unemotional when they underperform. All that means is the market wasn't conducive to their strategy at that time, but they will win long term. They always use the same, technical indicators to determine entries and exits, and they are able to trade many markets and stocks. They don't need to be experts on the fundamentals, like a Warren Buffett.

While discretionary traders are stressing about what the news means, strategic traders are reacting to current, actual market conditions. There is no opinion or prediction, just a predetermined, automated response from their proven strategies.

Clearly, the strategic approach is superior, but it's not easy to follow. You'll only follow your strategy if you believe in it deep down, psychologically.

Have you ever seen a day trader? They're stressed out of their mind, and most of them lose. The biggest reason people fail in trading is because their emotions commandeer their decision making. They haven't taken the time to define their beliefs and strategies and program them into an automatic process. They have some ideas, maybe some great ideas, but there's no way they can overcome their emotions and act consistently, as the markets move up and down, and the pundits scream and shout.

This is why I ignore the news and let my computer do the work for me. Computers don't feel stress; let them handle the grunt work.

You put in work up front. What do you get?

You no longer need a nine-to-five job. No more rat race—you're set for life, financially. You can live and work where you want. You can travel wherever you want, whenever you want, and still make money every day, with just thirty minutes of daily maintenance.

You don't have to open a newspaper, read expensive newsletters, or watch TV.

You spend time with family and friends, doing what you want.

It's real, it's what I do, and I'm going to show you how I do it.

I started trading in 2000 while helping manage my family's large retirement account, which was completely invested in a fundamental trading approach. It was managed by a high-profile wealth management bank in the Netherlands, in a huge, wonderful, classic, expensive building.

I saw the fancy building and people and couldn't help but

think, *Wow, they must be smart.* I saw all the money behind it and met with the manager; they had so much knowledge, as well as massive research reports. In the beginning, I was overwhelmed and impressed, like most people. But I started monitoring that account right after the dot-com boom had ended, and in two or three months, these huge accounts had lost about 30 percent.

I started to second-guess these big and fancy wealth management companies. In my next meeting with the wealth managers, I challenged them: "We're down 30 percent, et cetera, and it's not good." "Well, Laurens, the market is down, so you just need to wait it out, because the market will always go up in the long term."

I asked a reasonable question. "What is that logic based on?" They didn't have an answer. And then they told me to buy *more stocks*, because that would lower the average purchase price of the stocks we currently owned. They said, for example, we had purchased a stock at $100, and now it was down 30 percent, to $70. They said, buy the same amount, again, at $70, because your average price will be $85 and the stock only needs to move up 15 dollars to be back at even.

But every time we bought, they received more commissions!

These companies were trying to manipulate the market, telling all of their customers to buy, hoping to bring the market up, and taking their commissions regardless. But at the time, market sentiment was horrible. I didn't believe in what they were doing, and it was clear they just wanted us to buy so they'd get commissions.

I spoke to my father, who owned the account. We had too much risk exposed. We couldn't be invested completely in such bad times, I said. I recommended my father sell the entire account. We didn't know what we were doing, and we were relying on people who didn't care about how much money we made or lost, but rather the status of their commissions.

I convinced him, so we sold the entire portfolio. It had Enron and WorldCom in it, which both went bankrupt. We would've lost over 70 percent of our family's retirement account if we had held on to our positions, and even more if we had doubled down like the "experts" had recommended.

That proved to me that wealth managers weren't as smart as they preached, but I didn't yet know what I was doing. I just knew not to trust them.

Convincing the banks to liquidate our positions was a huge step, but all it did was take us from losing money to being flat. Making zero money wasn't good, either.

I started trading with a $30,000 account. I thought that by following the news I could guess exactly where the market was going. I had expensive software giving me up-to-date news, earning reports and Fed reports. I thought that the faster I had information, the faster I could take action and beat everyone else. I'd stare at my computer all day, nervously analyzing every piece of information as it was released. How would it affect my positions? I prayed for favorable news, glued to TV, radio, and the Internet. I needed every piece of information, or I'd be missing out.

I was constantly anxious. I smoked fifty cigarettes a day.

My account was swinging up and down, and it crushed me psychologically. I had health issues. I couldn't sleep. I was nervous, kept to myself, and lost self-esteem. I couldn't accept the fact that I was losing in the markets. I knew things were bad, but I didn't know what to do.

Eventually, I accepted that bankruptcy was coming, and the long road of educating myself began. I've now read over five hundred trading books, after years of six to eight hours of daily study. Not a day passed that I wasn't working on learning about the markets. I attended seminars and talked to any smart people I could find.

One day, I stumbled across a free book online which told the story of a group called the "turtles" who were taught to trade a simple, proven strategy from professionals. It turned out that the ones who followed the rules 100 percent made the most money. It had nothing to do with decision-making or analysis; the ones who followed the system closest made the most money. It was so simple, and made so much sense, but was so profound. That was my first breakthrough.

The second was that I found a style that really resonated with my personality: mean reversion. Basically, you buy a stock that is well oversold, which means it has a statistically larger likelihood than random to revert back to its mean (go back up in price). You have an edge when you trade like that consistently, long term. I hired a programmer and said, "Here are my ideas. Can you program this into an automated strategy?" Then I tested the strategy, and I had been correct. I was on to something. I had an edge. I started to trade and make money.

Later, my beliefs evolved, and I currently trade both mean reversion and trend following, combined.

Once I started making money, I could buy more specific educational material. I learned about every indicator, statistic, and piece of quantified evidence I could. I eyeballed thousands of stocks, guessed good entry and exit points, wrote them down, and tried to create proven rules. It was insanely difficult—I had no programming or back-testing experience. I just knew to look for something that consistently made money long term, because then I'd have an edge.

Hiring my first programmer was that first big breakthrough, but it was difficult. I had ideas, but I needed to explain them to my programmer, and make sure they were doable. It was a long, expensive road before I figured something out. I paid people by the hour, to work on slow computers, from 2005 to 2007. I didn't have millions of dollars for fancy computers—normal computers were slow to crunch numbers back then. Now, all you need is a decent laptop.

Back tests used to take twenty-four hours, if the computer didn't crash. Now, they take ten minutes. I was so convinced this would be where my edge lay, though, that I never gave up. Eventually, I created codes and strategy and defined exact parameters. My opinions turned out to be right: There was a real edge in strategic trading.

I was busy at the time and had to trade everything myself. Eventually, though, I improved my software and made the process less time-consuming.

Everybody doubted me. My friends, colleagues, and the

media told me I had to listen to the banks and experts. They told me I was full of crap, or a dreamer. It was tough to bear the criticism, but I believed in my philosophy. Even when 99 percent of my surroundings were laughing at me, I kept going.

I haven't smoked a cigarette in ten years, and I haven't had a losing year since 2007. My returns have been in the large double-digits.

My trading has evolved, and edges have decreased slightly over time as the market has gotten smarter, but I've also begun to combine strategies. For every strategy, there are market types for which the strategy won't work. When you have a sideways market, trend following does not work. You buy and sell with a loss. You get whipsawed. But mean reversion works great in a sideways market, and at most times, more than 70 percent of the market is trading sideways.

If you trade those two concepts together, plus multiple others, you'll always have a couple of strategies that work in current market conditions. Depending on one approach is risky, because no matter how smart you are, you can never predict which type of market is coming with perfect accuracy.

When markets are going down, you take the mirror of what I just wrote—you trade short trend following and short mean reversion, and you make money even when the markets are falling, because your long strategies are out of the market, and your short strategies are in, making money.

It all comes down to statistics and psychology; you have to understand your own unique psychology and risk management. My journey has taken me to many courses and seminars, resulting in serious psychological transformation and a feature in Van Tharp's latest book, *Trading Beyond the Matrix*. I wrote a chapter on my trading experiences, and how I transformed from a loser, following the masses, to a long-term winner, following my well-programmed computers.

I currently run a small investment fund where I manage money for institutional traders from the United States and Switzerland. More importantly, I have additional time to do what I love—mentoring people to create their own automated trading strategies, which eventually lead to financial freedom. This book exists so you can do that, too.

CHAPTER 2

The Thirty-Minute Trader

As we'll show in part 2, typical investment advisors use the crystal-ball technique called *fundamental analysis*, which is risky and suboptimal for long-term profit. My approach is quantified and automated—the complete opposite. My strategies completely ignore fundamental numbers.

Fundamental traders guess the future. These traders analyze earnings reports and other company numbers, and predict where the price will go based on their analysis. They have a conceptual idea of where the market will go, and then they make predictions. For example, they might say, "The economy is slowing down, so stock prices will probably go down."

Basically, it's the Warren Buffett model of investing. That sounds great, except that it's highly skill based. Buffett is the master in picking the right stocks, and few people are able to learn that skill. They think they can, but when they actually try to pick stocks, they fail. The common anecdote goes like this: If the average investor compared his results to a monkey choosing ten different stocks, the monkey would do better on average.

Picking random stocks beats the average investors' skill, because picking stocks is incredibly difficult, random, and counterintuitive. Using Buffett's strategy to pick stocks would be like using LeBron James's strategy to play basketball. Sure, slam dunking every play sounds like a nice strategy in theory, but if the average guy tried it, he would fall on his face. You need Buffett's otherworldly skill, decades of experience, and hours of daily hard work if you want to attempt his strategy.

It's also difficult for fundamental traders to create strict rules for when to buy and sell, because their discipline is so instinctive and skill based. Quantifying their exact decisions for when to buy and sell is therefore mostly impossible. They make a trade because they expect a certain outcome—that a company is going to do well. But what if they're wrong? Even the best traders will be wrong frequently. They don't have an exit strategy, because they're simply making a bet that a company will do well, and when it doesn't, they still expect things to turn around eventually.

Additionally, fundamental traders don't tend to have a strategy for when there is a big downturn. Whenever market sentiment is down, their accounts are down, too. They attempt to spread risk by investing in different companies and sectors; however, their complete exposure is long. Therefore, even though they are "diversified," their assets are correlated; they go up and down together. When the entire market sentiment is negative, *all sectors* go down. Diversification sounds nice in theory, but if all of your exposure is long, you will go down with the market.

When you most need protection, sector diversification won't help you. In bad times, your "diversified" stocks go down together, and you suffer.

By that, I mean this: Investors think that a diversified portfolio will protect them from catastrophe. That's not true, because diversification only applies to *sectors*, not market types. When there is a bad bear market and the markets are down, *all sectors go down*. All sectors are correlated in bear markets. Diversification works somewhat in bull markets—some sectors will do better than others—but when market sentiment is down, diversification is useless. Your entire portfolio will go down. I call this concept "Lockstep". It's when emotional responses create the mood in the market that everything is now going the other way and correlations are either 1.00 (perfectly correlated with zero diversification) or -1.00 (perfectly inversely correlated which means that you can't make any profits)

That's what happened in 2008. It didn't matter how you had diversified your portfolio—all of your "diversified" stocks went down together, and you suffered.

Once in a while, fundamental traders will be right, and it will pay outsized dividends. Often, they'll be painfully wrong, like with gold, as I'll explain in a moment. Over the past seven years or so, writers have been saying the US economy is in bad shape. The government is trillions of dollars in debt, and so on, which is true. It *is* in incredibly bad shape. However, that doesn't tell you exactly what will happen to stock prices in the coming year, because the emotions of traders are what control stock prices. You can't predict exactly *when* the inevitable downturn will occur, nor its magnitude. It could happen in a day, a month, a year, or a decade, and it could be of any size.

In 2011, gold was at $1,900, and I have never seen more newsletters start to say, "The world's going to end; the financial system is going to collapse; you must buy gold!" They reasoned that "gold always holds its value and maintains its purchasing power," "we might even go back to gold standards," and so on, and "then the price of gold will explode!"

Conceptually, there is truth in this analysis. The people who said it are not stupid. Yet from 2011 to 2015, gold dropped from $1,900 to $1,050, almost 50 percent! While the fundamental analysis made conceptual sense, and implied that gold would rise dramatically, the price action told you something different. Price action is all that matters.

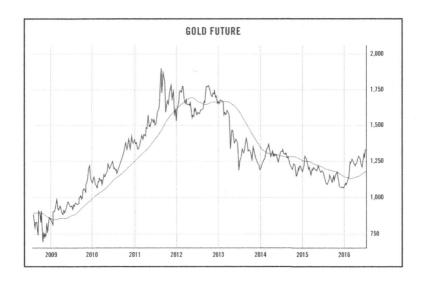

The standard, fundamental analysis (touted by many newsletters and media) would have lost you almost 50 percent on the big recommendation of gold, but a simple, long-term trend-following model would have told you otherwise. That model simply closes the position whenever it's below the two-hundred-day simple-moving average, so you would have gotten out around $1,600.

As usual, the white noise of newsletters and media was wrong, and a simple, technical exit based on price action would have saved you from disaster.

If I were trading a long-term, trend-following strategy, I would have definitely been in a long position on gold at $1,900, like the fundamental traders. However, technical analysis gives you clear rules on an exit plan. That's the key. You can be in a position that will eventually go bust, but you'll get out before it goes bust, because you're prepared.

There will be a moment where the computer measures the trend and tells you, "In this situation, historically, prices start to go down." It will tell you: "Based on past statistical evidence, this price is broken. Let's get out of here and eliminate our position on gold." Your balance would be saved.

Under a trend-following approach, you stay until the trend flips. Your technical strategy makes you far better off, because it understands that you must never be overconfident in your analysis, because all that matters is what prices the market displays. Fundamental traders, however, don't have that safeguard against overconfidence.

It wouldn't have mattered which specific trend-following approach you used. Any approach would have saved you from catastrophe, forcing you to exit as soon as the trend was measured over. All that matters is that you measure price action, and base your buying and selling decisions on that. That's the key.

Simple-moving averages (SMA), as I'll show in part 4, are a tenet in the philosophy of trend following. It's simple. When the computer tells you, based on SMA, that a trend is over, you exit. (See Ch. 4 for an example with Enron.)

You can analyze the fundamentals all you want, but the stock market is controlled by market sentiment. If the market doesn't agree with your analysis, you'll lose, even if your analysis was logically sound. That's why I focus solely on price action. It's the best measure of market sentiment that exists.

Another example of fundamental traders failing was in early 2009, with the S&P 500. We had just experienced the large bear market in 2008, and in March 2009, that bear market hit its low. From then on, the S&P 500 went up in price. In mid-2009, my trend-following strategies recognized buying signals, based on that price action. However, fundamental traders were still in a negative headspace, thinking, *The economy does not look good, therefore I'm not optimistic.* But if they had simply followed price action, the charts would have shown them that sometime in the summer or fall of 2009, they could've again entered positions. From then on, the S&P more than doubled in value.

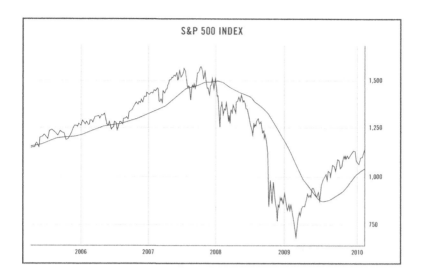

Fundamental traders cried about the massive national debt and other issues, yet the S&P tripled in value from its low in 2009. If you had completely ignored the fundamentals and all of the market's issues, and simply followed price action, you would have done incredibly well.

Technical analysis analyzes the past. Technical analysis completely ignores fundamentals, and looks at price action instead. My strategies analyze the historical price movements of the market, in order to find statistical edges. There are patterns that will repeat themselves in the long run, and if you trade according to these patterns, consistently, you will have an edge and beat the market. You don't *predict* the markets, like typical advisors do. That's nearly impossible; the market is too unpredictable. You simply *react* to the movements of the markets, once they happen. The key difference is that your strategy, based on past statistics, can accurately describe the market sentiment in numerical form and tell you what that sentiment means for future price action. You wait for the market to tell you something, and then you react based on your proven strategy.

Basically, the strategy quantifies how people are feeling about the market, based on price action. But it does this all with long-term, statistical significance—any pattern that hasn't been proven over a large sample size (which is quite common) is ignored. All recommendations are a combination of sound logic programmed into the strategy, plus statistical analysis.

My approach works, because we use statistical evidence based on real past historical price action data. Using price action data allows you to react according to the market. You may own a company's stock that looks good fundamentally, but if market sentiment isn't good, the price will go down.

You could have owned the greatest company in the world in 2008, with healthy earnings ratios and the like, but market sentiment would have killed you. All stocks went down, on average, 50 percent. Your fundamental analysis could have been perfect, but you would have lost half of your value because your exits weren't based on price action. That's the danger of working with fee-based advisors.

If you don't look at price action for a stock, you have no idea where the price is going. That's why I advise all of my clients to build their strategies based on price action. For the past fifteen years, I've trained myself to ignore fundamentals, while all of the "experts" who want your money do the opposite.

My approach is a quantified, technical approach. It is simply creating a proven strategy, and then following that strategy.

Once you have this strategy (and I will teach you proven ones), you do not need to have any skill. You follow the strategy. Fundamental trading can work if you have tremendous skill, but most people, myself included, do not have this skill. Unless you're Warren Buffett, fundamental trading is incredibly risky, and not particularly smart.

In the end, the computer program uses a strategy with a scientifically proven edge and predefined entry and exit rules that are based on historical performance. The rules tell you exactly what to do: when to buy, sell, and sit still. All you have to do is follow its instructions, like in the earlier example about gold.

Your computer is following a strategy of proven rules based on how investments have behaved in the past, and it knows when to cut losses short. It eliminates the risk of ruin inherent in fundamental traders' recommendations, which put too much stock in risky, unscientific predictions. Technical trading is the complete opposite of guesswork. It is quantified technical analysis of past price data. It only looks at price action, because that is the most accurate measure of market sentiment, which is the best predictor of stock prices. Everything is back tested, so every rule in the computer has a proven scientific edge over the benchmarks that wealth managers hope and pray to beat with their crystal balls.

My strategies use historical price action data, but there is a huge variety in each strategy type. A classic one is trend following. We cover many styles, but this is the easiest and simplest to start with. The data identifies stocks that are trending up. When they're trending up, you have the belief that when you enter that trade and buy, you will ride that trend until it's over. The data tells you when to stop, and at that moment, you cut your losses short. You get out of the trade, because the price action is telling you that the company's *sentiment* is not good anymore, regardless of its actual quality.

It's no longer the misleading news messages that tell you if a company is good or bad. The price tells you. If the price goes up, it's a good company. If the price goes down, it's a bad company. You'll get out, because otherwise, you'd lose money.

Still, there is no better option than using past data. Would you rather look into a crystal ball, or use beliefs based on the statistical proof that would have made money in the past? As long as you test your trading hypotheses and beliefs and prove them to be true and based on sound market concepts, you should make money over the long run.

Most importantly, using an automated strategy takes the emotion out of what can be an emotional business.

A quantified strategy means you defer to your computer. Every day, it tells you what to buy and sell. The computer's recommendations are rooted in *your beliefs*, because they are programmed into the computer. You're simply outsourcing the number crunching, and you get clear directions on exactly what to do. Your decisions are not based on predictive hunches— where you *think* the market is going. They're based on proven strategies, *reactions* to what the market tells you about current conditions.

Emotions are the number-one reason people fail in the stock market, but in my strategies, emotions play zero impact on your decision making. It's impossible for a human to behave like a rational computer on a day-to-day basis—but it's pretty darn easy for a computer to behave like a computer.

The key, though, is using multiple strategies in concert with each other. You can't focus only on trend following, for example. My trading plan works because it uses a suite of noncorrelated strategies—all traded simultaneously—so money can be made in every type of market. Mean reversion is the opposite of trend following, and yet it works great when the two are combined. That's because when one strategy is struggling, the other strategy makes up for it. I'll explain this in depth in part 4, when you learn how to set up your own strategy.

The idea is this: You trade different strategies, with different purposes, at the same time. There are three basic directional states a market can be in: bull market, bear market, and sideways market. We can further define based on volatility, but for this example we'll stick with direction. When you have a long-only strategy, like fundamental traders, you'll do well in bull markets, but you won't make money in sideways markets (the markets aren't moving). You'll also lose money in bear markets, like in 2008 when the S&P 500 dropped 56 percent and the NASDAQ dropped 74 percent. The bad times will wipe out all of the good times.

Perfect execution of a suite of noncorrelated strategies would look as follows. We start with a strategy that makes money when the market goes up: long-term trend following. That strategy will thrive only when we are invested in long positions. When the trends start to bend, those positions will be stopped out until we're going flat. Another type of strategy that works well in bull markets is a mean-reversion long strategy.

But the market will go down at some point, and your long positions will lose. That's why you'll be trading a short-selling strategy at the same time—to prepare for bear markets. It's a hedge strategy, ensuring that you'll make money when the market turns and goes down. Of course, you need to make sure you're not giving too much back with this hedge strategy, because it will lose money when the market is going up. But that's all covered in my strategies, as I'll explain.

It's an insurance premium, basically. You need to pay it to make sure that when the market goes down, you're covered. In a good year, when the market is going up, your long strategies will make great money, and your short-selling strategy will lose a little bit. But if another 2008-like situation happens, or even to a smaller degree like early this year (2016), your insurance will pay off and you'll end the year positive. At the same time, fundamental traders will be losing big.

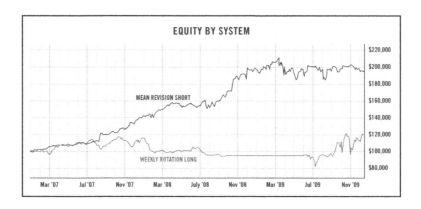

In the previous graph, we can clearly see a few things. At the end of 2007, the Weekly Rotation strategy (grey line) started to lose money, dropping about 25 percent. However, at the same time, our short-selling strategy (black line) made up for that with large profits.

In mid-2009, the situation reversed. The markets entered an uptrend, meaning the Weekly Rotation strategy (grey line) kicked in, and we started to execute a lot of long-term trades, making great money. The short-selling strategy (black line) lost a tiny bit. Overall profits were large.

That covers bear and bull markets, but there are also sideways markets, in which trend-following strategies don't generally work. However, we don't suspend those strategies. We are always trading every strategy simultaneously, because we want to be prepared for all unexpected market types. Therefore, we need strategies that work in sideways markets. Those are mean reversion strategies.

Mean reversion strategies are virtually the opposite of trend-following strategies. They buy the fear and sell the greed. If a stock is oversold, that means there has been a lot of panic regarding that stock. According to a mean-reversion strategy, that moment of panic is the perfect moment to buy that stock, because there is a statistically larger than random likelihood it will revert back to its mean price once the panic has subsided. Once the price returns to its mean, you exit the stock again. The strategy works in reverse, too. When there is a lot of greed in the market and stocks are overbought (there are too many bulls in the market), that's a good moment to sell greed. The reason is that there's a statistically larger chance than random that the market will react to the downsides.

You're buying the fear, because it has gotten so extreme that it has become a low-risk idea to invest, even though prices are going down. More than likely, things will turn around. This is based on a large sample of statistics. Sample size is key. If it were based on, say, thirty trades, the statistical likelihood of your hypothesis being true would be tiny. But when it's based on scientific proof from three thousand trades, your likelihood is high, and in the long run, you'll win.

Of course, you'll also do the inverse, which is selling greed.

You're still looking at price action. With trend following, you look for a certain indicator which says, "Okay, now the price is trending up." With mean reversion, you look for price action to tell you a stock is oversold, so that it's becoming cheap. (With short selling, it's vice versa.) Perhaps the stock has been moving down for the last four days, 15 percent or more. The simple price action rule, if tested and proven, might be, "If I buy every stock that over the last four days has dropped 15 percent or more in value, then there is a statistically larger than random chance that it will revert back to its mean. Therefore, if I trade this strategy consistently, I'll make significant profits in the long term." That means you have an edge, and we only trade when we have a statistically proven edge. Generally, mean reversion is shorter term and is buying fear, or the opposite, selling greed.

As you can see, combining strategies ensures that we'll make money regardless of how the market is performing. We do this because virtually no one can predict what the market will do with reasonable accuracy. We take that variable out of the equation, depending only on our proven strategies, rather than the unpredictable whims of the market. We accept that picking stocks is only for geniuses like Warren Buffett who devote their life to it, and build a computer program around our deficiencies as humans. Humans are good at many things, but in this case, it's smart to let a computer do all of the grunt work. We aren't fortune-tellers, and we can't crunch numbers like computers.

Often, people have long-only or open positions, so when the market turns sour, they freak out. Everything on TV and online is bad, scary news, and they can't help but react. People are basing their decisions on what other people tell them is fundamentally good, and then they get anxious about their positions. Of course, you don't need to listen to the news if you have an automated strategy that is prepared for any market type—bull, bear, or sideways! Your task is simply to follow your strategy, because it is *designed* to make money in all market types. The news becomes irrelevant.

Imagine a scenario like 1929-1932, when your account would have dipped lower by the day. The Dow Jones and S&P 500 lost more than 80 percent of their value! If a time like that ever happens again, you'll be grateful that you're trading both long and short, and not exposing yourself to those losses. By designing a strategy that works well in both up and down markets, you've won the game. Your mental state will never be affected by inevitable downturns in the market. You can finally relax, as your money increases long term.

Investing is my life's work, and I'm still often wrong in my personal predictions. For example, after the big bear market in 2008, around March 2009, many people were still writing that the world was going to end, like in 1929. They said it would go down another 30 percent. I actually agreed with that opinion, thinking the worst wasn't over. But when you least expected it, and there was extreme fear, the market started to rise again. People's logical thoughts and beliefs said one thing, but the price of the market said exactly the opposite. The prices are all that matter.

If I had followed my beliefs and opinions like most people do, I would have lost money. But I trusted my strategy, which ignores my personal predictions in favor of my suite of non-correlated strategies. My bull strategies were already in place and trading, and I made money. By automating things and removing your opinions and beliefs from the equation, you make money even in the common instance that the market doesn't make sense to you. The stock market is wholly unpredictable, so we plan around that, and make money regardless of what happens. We don't hope to be right; we defer to the unpredictability of the market. What we're doing is lowering our expectations but winding up with a better result. We're ignoring our natural cockiness and ego, being rational instead, and profiting in the end.

Now, how do you create your own, personalized strategy? As I've explained, you base it on your beliefs, but not your predictions. The difference is that beliefs are ideas that can be back tested against historical price action; they are beliefs about what the market historically does when it is performing a certain way. Predictions are different and are based on evaluating individual companies, rather than reacting to the entire market on a broad level. It's nearly impossible to predict individual stocks, because they are so dependent on market sentiment. It is entirely possible, however, to understand what current market conditions mean for all stocks, when calculations are automated to a powerful computer.

However, not all strategies are the same. Your strategy needs to be tailored to your unique situation. You do the work beforehand (which I'll describe in depth in part 3) to reflect yourself in your strategy. You start with the core market concepts I have explained and will continue to explain: trading long and short at the same time, and trading both trend following and mean reversion. Therefore, you're covered regardless of what the market does. You don't need to predict what the market will do, because you're covered in all scenarios. Within that framework, though, you will define your own personal beliefs and preferences. Then you trade according to your strategy, responding to the market's price action, rather than riskily predicting it.

If your beliefs are different than mine, your strategy will look different. But as long as you have a clear understanding of core market principles, both of our strategies will work. For example, my suite of twelve noncorrelated strategies doesn't work for people who have IRA or 401K accounts, because those restrict you from trading short. The solution would be to set your beliefs as long-trading biased. You are mildly limited, but it would still be possible to make good money. The only difference would be that there will be times when your strategy is out of the market and flat, because your indicators are telling you it's currently a bear market. While my strategy would be making money, you would be flat. However, you would make more money in bull markets, because you aren't paying the insurance hedge of a short strategy.

(There are some options to work with buying inverse exchange-traded funds [ETFs] and thus having a hedge, but the structure of those products are often misleading, so you need to be careful.)

Once your strategy is created, you don't need to look at the news *at all*. Fed numbers came out? You don't care. Company reports, yearly profits, blah, blah, blah—you not only don't care about it, but you actively ignore it, spending time on things that enrich your life. You're simply following your strategy, which tells you when and what to enter and exit. You just follow what price action is telling your strategy to do. The computer does all of the work and tells you when to buy and sell.

It's no problem to trade three or four strategies at the same time. In fact, I trade up to twelve strategies simultaneously. This would be impossible to do without a computer, but my years of programming and testing thoughts and beliefs are now reflected in my automated strategy. Now, the analysis takes just a click on the computer. And because I only use end-of-day data, I can do my analysis in less than thirty minutes a day, and so can you. You can do it from anywhere in the world, because the only thing you need to do is wait until the market has closed, download your data, scan for the new trade setups, and then open your broker platform and make sure that before the market opens again, you enter the trades.

You can do this without any emotion clouding your judgment, because your task is not to be smart and pick the right stocks. It's nearly impossible to outsmart the market. Your task is to follow the strategy, which anyone can do. You don't care what the market is doing, because you have strategies in place to profit regardless of how it performs, no matter of how unexpected.

Most people lose money when they let their emotions get the best of them. As humans, we can't be levelheaded and rational all the time, especially while losing money. For that reason, you program your risk tolerance into your strategy. The maximum money you can stomach losing is predetermined. Your strategy will tell you to stop trading at that threshold. Many people build a good strategy, but as soon as it goes down 5 percent or 10 percent, they freak out, lose trust, and make bad decisions. If you define your maximum drawdown beforehand, you'll stay calm and collected. You'll be prepared for the worst, and you'll know exactly what the worst is.

For example, you may predefine that you're unwilling to lose more than 20 percent of your equity. When you compare that to the max drawdown of the S&P 500 (over 50 percent), that's not a large number. I define risk tolerance as your maximum drawdown. Someone may *say* losing 20 percent of their balance isn't a problem, but that answer isn't usually based on experience. I work with people to visualize this loss vividly, to check the accuracy of their answer. "You *say* you're OK with a 20 percent drawdown, but let's say your $1 million trading account is down to $800,000. Are you OK with losing $200,000?"

If you haven't visualized this potential loss, clearly defining the point where you will lose hope for long-term recovery, you'll override your strategy as soon as the inevitable downturn hits. That will end in catastrophe. You need to trust in your strategy's ability to recover, long term. If you've analyzed yourself enough to know what you can truly handle (and I'll explain how), then you'll know that big drawdowns are part of the game. You won't panic, because you know you need to risk money and lose it temporarily to make money long term. Yes, you'll make money consistently, in up and down markets, but there will still be times when the market is so bad that even with a perfect strategy, you'll lose money. You'll lose less than fundamental traders and virtually everyone, but you'll still lose. You need to be able to stomach losses and trust your strategy's long-term, scientifically proven results.

Now, what do you have to do before creating your own strategy to achieve financial independence in thirty minutes a day? First, you need to take serious time to analyze yourself, so you deeply understand your personality, preferred lifestyle, and trading beliefs and preferences. You may not like shorting stocks, for example. That's fine, but if you don't account for that when creating your strategy, you'll have trouble following your computer's orders, and you'll fail. You need to be honest with yourself and make sure you'll follow your strategy. You can only trade according to your beliefs. Those beliefs must reflect sound, proven market principles, but they also must suit your individuality. There are plenty of sound principles, so not everyone needs to trade the same strategies.

For example, if you are impatient, trend following is going to be difficult to follow. You will have long positions that will last for two or three months without profit. You wait a long time, see no results, then make a big profit. It's effective, but boring. Impatient people will get bored and exit too soon. The profits don't come quickly enough. There's not enough action. You might believe in trend following, but your beliefs also must mesh with your personality, or it will be a disaster.

If you're following mean reversion, you must be able to ignore the news completely. I never watch the news. The principles for mean reversion are buy fear and sell greed. If you watch the news, it's difficult not to be influenced by experts shouting. You need to buy when there is a lot of panic in the market. You go against the herd and the shouting. That is not for everybody, nor is the opposite (selling greed). Mean reversion is the opposite of trend following, where you follow the whims of everyone. If you're not comfortable ignoring mainstream opinion and going against the herd, you're going to struggle trading mean reversion.

It's also key to incorporate your preferred lifestyle into your strategy. If you want a life where you only need to watch the market thirty minutes a day, there's a strategy for that, like the one I use. If you only want to watch the markets once a week, there's a different strategy. If you only want to watch the markets once a month, there's a strategy for that. If you love activity and want to make ten to fifty trades a day, there's a strategy for that. I have students with busy jobs, traveling around the world as big-time executives, and they don't even have time for those thirty daily minutes. But they incorporate that into their strategies, and do great. Each strategy works as long as it is clearly defined beforehand, so it will be followed precisely, with no trouble, doubt, or panic.

You put in the hard work beforehand to create a strategy and set of rules that you know you can follow, long term, and then you simply follow them and profit. As long as you're honest and diligent up front, you'll have tremendous success. The only way to fail is to fail to be honest with yourself.

Before we continue, it's important to understand what we're up against. Financial institutions will tout their performance versus the benchmark, often the S&P 500, but more than 80 percent of institutional traders fail to beat it. That is mainly due to commissions, fees. Here's a visual look at the S&P's performance since 1995.

JAN 2, 1995 – NOV 23, 2016	BENCHMARK
CAGR	7.45%
Maximum Drawdown	56.47%
Annualized Volatility	19.28%
Longest Drawdown	86.1
Sharpe	0.39
MAR	0.13
YTD Return	8.25%
MTD Return	3.83%
Total Return	381.79%

As you can see, the benchmark has been far from impressive, with an average compound annual growth rate (CAGR) of 7.37 percent, a maximum drawdown of 56 percent, and two large drawdowns that lasted over five years. If you had started at an equity high like in 2000 or 2007, you would have entered in a drawdown, and waited over five years to get back to the breakeven point. Not good.

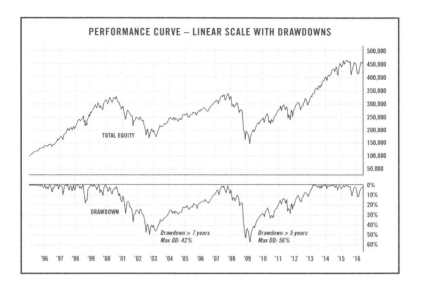

Since 2009, the benchmark (and stock indices in general) has done well, so buy-and-hold approaches have worked. This is a problem, because it causes people to look at the recent future and forget the past. The next big downturn, like 2000, 2002, or 2008, is just a matter of time. It *will* happen, at some point, so we need a strategy in place to survive.

Looking at the previous chart, it's obvious that buying a mutual fund that tracks or closely correlates to the index is unwise, because you will lose half of your equity when the downturn hits. What if you started with a million dollars, and now you're suddenly at $500,000? Will you still trust that your money comes back?

In the following chapter, I'll show you how to set up simple strategies, based on fundamentally correct trading principles, following simple indicators. My purpose isn't to show you how smart or great I am. My purpose is to show you that beating the market can be simple, if you know what you're doing and ignore mainstream financial advice.

PART 2

Beating the "Experts"

CHAPTER 3

The "Experts" Are Stealing Your Money

If you turn on the TV or read the news, you can't help but think that investing is treacherous and time-consuming, and that you need to hire an expert to manage your accounts. Daily financial media throws complicated numbers at you, so wealth managers swoop in and promise to hold your hand and make you money. They say, "If you don't know the earning reports and insider numbers, you'll never pick the best stocks to hold long term. You don't have the time, information, or expertise, so hire an expert!" It's overwhelming, disempowering, and confusing.

It's also complete nonsense.

Most people hire wealth managers via the typical, fee-based advisor system. But this system is designed to make *them* money, through your commissions. It's not designed to maximize benefits for *you*, individual investors.

You hire a big firm, and they charge you a yearly fee to control your investments. They also charge you transaction fees for when they buy and sell your stocks and tweak your portfolio, plus performance fees.

They virtually all use the same strategy: buy and hold. Pick stocks, and stick with them, long term. Their goal is to beat the market indices, like the S&P 500. They mostly use what is called *fundamental analysis*. They look at a bunch of numbers, like earnings reports, and guess where each particular stock is headed. There is no clear exit strategy, nor is there scientific evidence that buy and hold works. Big firms justify their logic by saying, "The market always goes up in the long run." But as anyone who has witnessed the market's multiple crashes knows, the market inevitably sees big drops, and it doesn't always recover.

This was exactly the case in both 1929 and 2008, and the results were disastrous. The 1929 crash led to a bear market that continued until 1932. As shown in the following chart, if we assume that people started to invest at the equity high (~380), they would have seen a drawdown of 88 percent, and it would have taken twenty-five years for them to fully recover their losses. Of course, most people wouldn't have the patience to wait twenty-five years. When people see big drawdowns, they generally run away from their advisors and quit trading for at least five to ten years, holding their extreme losses.

When you don't have a complete strategy that prepares for bad times, your emotional state will dictate your decisions. In bad times, you'll liquidate your portfolio at the worst possible time, and be forced to live with your losses forever. You'll sell, not based on a strategic decision, but rather by the sight of your bleak bank account. This happens to almost every trader.

It happened to me, before I woke up and realized I needed to prepare for these inevitable bad times. The solution is an automated strategy that trades both long and short simultaneously. Without a clear strategy in place beforehand, drawdowns are impossible to recover from, because you'll liquidate before the market goes back up.

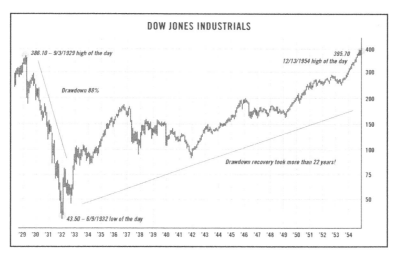

When the markets go down (and they always will), your portfolio, if you're invested in a buy-and-hold strategy, goes down with it. Also, since big firms have so many clients, they can't advise on lower-volume stocks. Trading lower-volume stocks with a massive client base would impact the market and evaporate any edge. They're forced to only recommend large companies, which means their model loses just as much as the general industries.

Also, they only make money when you have money in the market.

When the market crashed in 2008, and the S&P was down 56 percent, the firms kept your money in the market, as your balance tanked. If they had taken your money out, as a smart investor would have done, they wouldn't have received any commissions. The firms are controlling your money, but have different incentives than you. Would you give your car keys to a fast driver who would bill you for any damages *he* inflicted?

When the market crashes, advisors will say: "Yeah, you're down 45 percent, but the index is down 56 percent! We're actually doing well, relatively. The market will go up long term, and you'll make your money back." They don't know when the market will go back up, though, or by how much, and you're forced to deal with the stress of losing your hard-earned savings in the meantime. You may never see that money again. They'll tell you, "You just have to deal with this." They make you believe that it's "part of the game," that this is normal and happens to every investor. It's not, as you'll learn in this book.

Of course, you don't have to deal with this, because your money should have been out of the market. You only have to deal with a tanking balance if you hand your money to someone without skin in the game. There is no guarantee your balance will turn around. The "experts" are lying to you, because they have a different agenda—they want commissions.

And the thing is, when you add up all of the hidden fees, *more than 90 percent of advisors don't even beat the index.* Advisors need a huge staff to conduct their complicated analysis, and they pass that cost off to you, through management and transaction costs, and sometimes performance fees. If you bought the index yourself, you wouldn't have paid any of these costs. You could have done what they're doing, on your own, for free.

The wealth management industry wants you to *depend on them*. They want you to think you can't invest on your own, even though you can. That the only people *in the know* are smart analysts from the big banks who can analyze company fundamentals, pick the right stocks for you, so you hold and profit forever.

But the analysts from big banks are not traders. They don't make a living buying or selling stocks. They make a living *recommending* stocks, writing what people want to read, and they don't have any skin in your game. They get their salary and that's it, regardless of how their recommendations perform.

Their job is to sound smart, look good, and convince you to hire them. They're good at that. They're not good at making you money. They get paid whether you win or lose. They get paid when they beat the index, even if the index is tanking, and you're losing half of your money. If they beat the index, they'll not only get paid, but they'll also get praise from their bosses, and bonuses, as your retirement funds vanish.

Hiring one of these firms would be like a basketball coach hiring a sportswriter to make his lineup decisions. "I'm sorry, Kobe Bryant, but a writer said that you aren't playing well, so you're not playing tonight." If the team lost, the writer would keep his job and his salary, but the coach would get fired. It sounds ridiculous, but that's how the financial world works.

Not only are advisors' incentives misaligned with yours, but their strategies are flawed.

In certain times, like bull markets or the recent up markets since 2009, their strategies will work. Those times are great for buy-and-hold strategies, but they aren't sustainable, because the market will inevitably shift. Sooner or later, it will end in catastrophe, like 1929 or 2008.

The good times, like right now (October 2016), are the most dangerous. The market has been on an uptrend since 2009, so buy and hold has outperformed most quantified strategies. That means inexperienced traders are convinced that buy and hold works, that stocks will always go up in the long run. The longer this happens, the more stupid capital will be invested in the market, and the larger the downturn will be when the happy days are over. Excess greed will cause the inverse reaction of excess fear, and the market will drop sharply.

Another example was after the dot-com boom. There was a bull market from March, 1995 to the early 2000s. Everybody was trading long in tech stocks, and making 30 to 50 percent a year, easily. Everything was going up. Then the NASDAQ dropped 80 percent in two years.

This trend has happened over and over. Don't get greedy. Prepare for the inevitable bad times, so that you don't lose your hard-earned savings.

Fundamental traders say, "This stock should be priced at X based on our fundamental analysis." Then they'll peer into their crystal ball, saying, "This company's management is good; therefore, their price will go up." But you don't know everything that's going on in a company from a few numbers. That's pseudoscience.

CHAPTER 4

Proof Automated Trading Works

A company's stock price is not determined by its fundamentals. A market, by definition, means prices are determined by money flowing in and out—supply and demand. This is decided by *the emotions of the traders and investors* who create the demand, or basic desire, to buy or sell the stocks. *A stock's price is the result of the aggregate perception of traders, not the company's fundamentals. If the market likes a company, its price goes up. It's as simple as that.*

You could have had the greatest company in the world in 2008, with healthy earnings ratios and the like, but market sentiment would have killed you. All stocks went down, on average, 50 percent. Your fundamental trading analysis could have been perfect, but you would have lost half of your value because your exits weren't based on price action.

If you use a fundamentals approach—"I believe in this stock," "I think management is good," or, "The price is going down, but that just means we can get a good price"—you'll have irrational confidence in holding a losing stock. If the stock keeps going down, like Enron in the 2000s, when the press told you to keep riding this "great stock that was so cheap," reality will hit you like a ton of bricks. You'll lose all of your money. Enron went to *zero*.

Without exits based on price action, you're forced to rely on company reports and the news. By ignoring price, you're exposed to the next potential Enron scenario. You can't wait until your stock drops 70 percent, and banks and analysts tell you to sell. That's far too late; you will have lost a fortune.

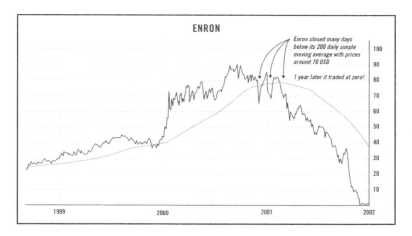

Price earnings numbers are based on earnings numbers, but if those reports don't reflect a clear and honest reality, which they often don't, those numbers are useless. They're often manipulated. Price action is real, yet it's ignored by most fundamental traders.

Any type of trend-following strategy (like the ones in the following example) would have saved you from staying in Enron until it was bankrupt. However, two brokerage firms, using fundamental analysis, RBC Capital Markets and UBS Warburg, didn't down-grade Enron from a "strong buy" until the stock had fallen from its fifty-two-week high of $84.87 to $4.14, in late 2001.

In the following table, you'll see nine different trend-following exits. None of these exits follows a magic formula—they're all simple, with one thing in common. They all follow price action. They ignore analyst reports and price-earnings ratios—the exit point is defined by looking at price action, nothing more.

Any one of these various exits would have prevented disaster easily. Some exit earlier, and some later, but the evidence is clear that *any* kind of simple price action would have saved you from catastrophe. Which one you chose wouldn't have mattered—the problem was that most people didn't have an exit strategy at all.

TREND-FOLLOWING EXITS	ENRON	DATE
Lowest low 200	63.50	03/12/2001
Lowest low 100	68.87	11/30/2000
MA 200	77.50	11/24/2000
50-200 Crossover	62.25	03/13/2001
30-100 Crossover	71.50	02/23/2001
15% Trailing Stop	67.40	03/1/2001
25% Trailing Stop	61.27	03/12/2001
3ATR Trailing Stop	73.80	02/21/2001
10ATR Trailing Stop	59.85	03/21/2001

What happens when the earnings information you're relying on isn't correct? Enron. Bankruptcy. You *must* base your trading decisions on price action. Fee-based advisors don't, and they therefore expose you to the risk of ruin.

Why would you pay someone money for a suboptimal strategy, where you bear all the risk, and they get paid even if you lose money?

You're smarter than that, which is why you've picked up this book.

I'm not here to sell you my expertise in picking stocks. That's not a winning strategy. My philosophy is that anyone can set up a winning, automated stock trading strategy that need not require more than thirty minutes of work a day. Your strategy will beat the market consistently, and employ varied strategies so that you'll make money even when the market is going down.

It involves using a quantified approach in which we define our trading decisions based on programming proven rules, based on historical price action data, into a computer, which then does all the grunt work for you. It's backward looking, based on statistical evidence, rather than forward looking, paying "experts" to peer into a crystal ball.

You'll be able to ignore misleading TV messages, because your computer will tell you exactly what to do. It takes the confusion and stressful emotions out of trading.

You'll have to work hard up front, in identifying and crafting the perfect strategy for you to make money long term. But I'll walk you through the process, step by step (this is what I do with my coaching clients), so that you won't need experts anymore and can make money on your own.

This is how the process works.

First, you **formulate a hypothesis of how the stock market works**. In order to trade successfully, you need a clear vision of your beliefs. Your beliefs are the core tenet to any successful trading strategy. Without clear beliefs, you won't be able to define rules nor trade a strategy successfully.

Next, you need to use those beliefs to **create a rule-based process of entry and exit criteria for which stocks to buy and sell**. Once your beliefs are clear and proven true based on sound market principles, they need to be quantified into specific rules. The more specific they are, the easier your trading.

Then, **this is all converted into an algorithm by a programmer, with back-testing software**. I hired a programmer to do this for me. The human mind is unable to process such large quantities of information on a daily basis, so you leave the computing to…a computer. You automate my beliefs and rules, and the computer evaluates them in a matter of minutes. Not only does it save time, but it evaluates without your natural human bias, which we all have. The computer does nothing but computes the strategy and spits out accurate data.

Next, **you need a historical data provider to back test your strategy**. In order to actually trade your strategy, you need scientific proof that it has an edge. Otherwise, you'll lose money. We need to first determine if there is an edge, then quantify it so that we know what to expect in the future.

Finally, **you optimize the combinations to get your desired results, and then determine whether or not it's tradable**. Once you have a data provider and your rules correctly coded, you define the exact parameters. There is a specific process for this, and it must be done correctly. The task is *not* to create parameters that show the best results, because past results don't guarantee future results. It could have been a coincidence. You need to test your parameters and see if they can be trusted to perform well in the future, too. Your strategy must be robust.

Once your strategy is created, implementation is easy. **Every day, you download the daily price updates.** Then, **you scan with your software and code (written for stocks that fit the criteria of your strategy)**. These two actions simply require clicking a few buttons. The computer does all of the work.

Every day, the software provides you with the buy and sell orders, automatically.

Then you simply enter the orders in your broker platform manually or in an automated way, and go about your day.

As you can see, the process can be divided into three areas:

1. Your beliefs of the stock market, and how you can make money
2. Programming and testing
3. Execution

This looks like a lot of work, but it's not. I began turning my beliefs into a strategy in 2007, and it has taken me a long time to perfect it, but once it's done, you have it for life. Creating your strategy is difficult work, but it grants you a lifelong asset.

Now, the whole trading process takes me less than thirty minutes a day. All I need to do is the execution part, clicking a few buttons and entering my orders into my brokerage platform.

You'll have to work hard up front, in order to identify and craft the perfect strategy for you to make money long term. But I'll walk you through the process, step by step (this is what I do with my mentoring clients), so that you won't need experts anymore—you can make money on your own.

PART 3

Building Your Perfect
Thirty-Minute Trading Strategy

CHAPTER 5

What It Takes—First, Know Thyself

To build your own thirty-minute trading strategy, you need to start by getting to know yourself. Who are you, in terms of trading? What's the optimal trading strategy for your personality? Are you impatient? Not at all? Are you a crowd follower, or an independent thinker? If you have one of those qualities, then what should you do about it, to compensate or take advantage?

There are three elements to knowing yourself. You must know your personality type, your edge, and your beliefs (which can be broken down into psychological beliefs, strategy beliefs, and position beliefs). You need to define yourself in each of these terms before creating your strategy. Otherwise, you're destined for failure.

Let's start with your personality type. Knowing yourself, and how your personality meshes with market principles, is essential. If you're impatient, you'll need to account for that. If you're disciplined, you can follow a higher-frequency trading strategy, but you'd better be sure you're *actually* disciplined. If you don't have the discipline to follow a daily routine, make sure you have a strategy to compensate for that. It may be smart to use a strategy that trades once a week, for example. If you want to watch the news every day, you need to understand the potential harm of that, and plan accordingly.

Trading success comes down to understanding and quantifying your edge versus the market. One of the biggest edges you can have is understanding yourself, and how your beliefs will reflect your trading. It's difficult, but it will pay massive dividends—literally.

We all know this stuff intellectually, but few people put in the work to understand themselves. The results are catastrophic. I know this, because I've made all of these mistakes. I had to learn the hard way, but you don't have to.

First, I learned to acknowledge the limitations of human nature. We all think we can avoid them, but we can't. It is, indeed, our *nature*. Here are some universal principles I've learned, through ignoring them all and suffering the consequences.

It goes against human nature to *ever* sell a stock at a loss. When you've lost money, human nature is to wait for the stock to rebound. It's the *sunk cost fallacy*; our brains don't want to admit we made a mistake. When you reframe the result to understand that it wasn't a *mistake*, but rather one small result in an overall sea of long-term profitability, you can let that go. No individual trade matters; what matters is the long-term result of thousands of trades. Selling at a loss isn't a bad thing, and it's often the best thing you can do. It means you saved yourself further losses, which could have destroyed your balance.

Next, decisions to sell should *never* be influenced by your initial buying price. Considering your initial price makes you fall prey to the *sunk cost fallacy*, or its reverse, thinking you haven't milked the stock for all its worth. It makes you lose objectivity and rational thinking.

This is easy to understand intellectually, but hard to follow in practice. Our emotions have more sway over our decisions than we care to admit. Most people refrain from selling a stock because they *don't want to close a position with a loss.* That's ridiculous. The market doesn't care how much you paid for a certain stock, so why let your entry price impact your buying and selling?

It's crucial to learn this all through real-world experience, because there's no way to simulate your emotional response to the unpredictability of the market. You need to know how it feels to win money, and more importantly, how it feels to lose money. You can read and study and think you know how to trade, but until you know how your psyche is impacted by constant losses (which everyone experiences), you are not ready to trade seriously. Start small, with money you can afford to lose. Treat it like an apprenticeship, or internship. Pay your dues, and learn through cheap failure. Otherwise, you're doomed to fail expensively. Overconfidence in stock trading can ruin your life.

I was *so naive* when I started. I had an initial base capital of $30,000, but I expected to earn $100,000 (or more) a year. That was ludicrous, and it led to impatience and overaggressive trading. I wasn't unique, though. Many people I work with think they can make 300 percent profits or more a year, not under-standing that aggressive trading comes with serious risk. I was undercapitalized, and it was the death of me.

Worse, I didn't have a plan or strategy. I just wanted to be Mr. Hotshot Trader. I needed clear and realistic objectives and goals, and a method of achieving them. I wanted to project a certain image to the outside world: a rich trader dominating this excit-ing, fast-paced world. It was nonsense. I needed a plan. I never defined which kind of strategy I would trade, or considered which strategy would suit me. Would I trade fundamentally, algorithmically, or through technical analysis?

I just sat at my screen every day, watched the news and charts, and bought when I thought prices would rise. I always put a stop in, but neither the buying decision nor the exit point was based on rational strategy. I was just guessing, but I convinced myself that with experience I'd be able to "feel" the movement, and then I'd be rich.

With an account of $30,000, I needed to take enormous risks in order to potentially make a living. My account rose and dropped 10 percent in a day, constantly, but I thought nothing of it. I thought I was close to finding the Holy Grail, that 100 percent correct strategy that would never fail.

I had no self-knowledge. I didn't know my strengths or weak-nesses; I didn't know who I was. Therefore, I had no idea what my edge was. I had no knowledge of psychology, and I did no work on myself. Trading is comparable to professional sports; you can only succeed with the proper mental state, training, and strategy. Trading is psychological warfare, yet I was going out there clueless. I had no chance at becoming a successful trader.

Now I can see that I wanted to trade because I had a lack of adventure in my life. I thought trading could fill that void while getting me rich. But through years of transforming my thoughts, beliefs, and psychology, I've learned that trading is the worst place to look for excitement and adventure. Looking for excitement in the markets is a virtual guarantee of failure. It's essential to have proper motives for trading. If you need adventure, find it elsewhere. That's why I do adventure sports and travel constantly.

It took me years to figure out how to build a successful strategy from the ground up. The truth is, a strategy built on sound trading concepts and your personal beliefs, with a relatively small Sharpe ratio (risk/reward measurement) of 1.5, is infinitely better than a strategy developed through rigorous back tests to find the "perfect" combinations. Sound beliefs and personalization matter more than anything, to ensure your strategy is sustainable and impervious to changing market conditions. A strategy based on beliefs is superior to any other, because when your trading setups are supported by your beliefs, you won't have trouble trading them. You'll actually follow your strategy.

Your one goal is to trade the strategy, but if your strategy isn't based on your actual beliefs, you will override the strategy when times get tough. Don't let that happen.

If you haven't traded before, you need access to a proven strategy (like the ones in part 4). Then you can simply execute it and learn as you go. Most people start trading and think they can come up with their own, unique strategies. That would be like someone reading four books on brain surgery and then stepping into the operating room. For brain surgery, fortunately, no one would let you into the operating room. For trading, though, access is easy. Open a brokerage account, and you'll get bonuses. That's to encourage you to trade, so brokers can get their commissions. Once you're in the game, it's hard to quit. Beginners are allowed to play with the pros, but they'll lose.

To start, write down everything you know about yourself, in terms of trading. Don't make the common mistake of evaluating yourself half-heartedly. It will destroy your financial future.

I'm a big fan of the Myers-Briggs personality assessment; knowing your type is essential before creating your strategy. This isn't so that you're put in a box and classified as a certain type of trader; it's so that you understand how your inborn personality will reflect in trading. Next, you'll identify the steps you can take to improve on your weaknesses.

Myers-Briggs is based on four dichotomies—each person leans toward one of the two options in each category. It's not all-or-nothing; it's simply a side you veer toward more.

First there is *extraversion* versus *introversion*. Next, there is *sensing* versus *intuition*, *thinking* versus *feeling*, and *judgment* versus *perception*. There are sixteen different personality types, determined by whichever combination of those four dichotomies the test says you prefer.

I haven't seen any difference between extroverts and introverts in terms of trading, but for the others, the differences are significant.

People who prefer *intuition* tend to see the big picture better than those who prefer *sensing*—the more detail-oriented bunch. For developing strategies, *intuition* is preferred.

As for *thinking* versus *feeling*—*thinking* has a huge edge. In trading, you can't make decisions with your heart.

Finally, *judging* types are more disciplined and better planners than *perceiving* types, who are more open-ended and dislike routine, discipline, and deadlines.

It's important to understand that these are simply preferences. You can work on your weaknesses, and you can win money trading even if you aren't the "ideal" trader. Also, your weaknesses in trading may be your strengths in other areas of life.

I'm a perceiving type, but I've worked on and account for this weakness. Once you accept it, you can overcome it. I hate working with a planned, nine-to-five routine; I work when I'm inspired. For that reason, I've outsourced and automated my trading. My programmer is the one that needs to be disciplined, and I hired him with that in mind. It's the perfect solution.

Thinking of the big picture comes easily to me, but I also have a slight tendency toward feeling rather than thinking. It's inborn. But I know that trading requires rational, objective thinking, so I have worked to step into that proverbial "thinking person" when I'm working. I've worked hard on that, and it has paid off.

Work on yourself to improve your weaknesses, and outsource what you struggle with. Your weaknesses are other people's strengths. They'll be happy to get paid to do what they're good at. If you're a feeling type, that's a weakness, but having 100 percent awareness of that fact is the most crucial thing you can do. Weaknesses can be overcome, but only once you admit them.

Take a Myers-Briggs test. If it turns out you have a weakness, accept it, realize it's a strength in other aspects of life, and put routines and rules in place so that it doesn't impact your trading.

Also, realize these aren't absolute. If you're a feeling or perceiving type, that's just a preference, an inclination. The first step to overcoming it is awareness. Next is looking for a solution: outsourcing, automation, transformation. It's possible to get more disciplined, by training yourself with things like Neuro-Linguistic Programming (NLP).

CHAPTER 6

The Beliefs All Top Traders Share

When you're trading in the markets, you're trading your beliefs. Therefore, accessing, identifying, and understanding your beliefs is essential.

The best traders use a wide variety of strategies—mean reversion, scalping, long-term trend following, short-term trading. They all can work under the right circumstances, for the right person. That said, there are a few common beliefs that *virtually all top traders share*, and they're essential to understand. Your strategies can vary, but you should pay close attention to these core beliefs.

Most importantly, top traders understand the importance of *having* beliefs. That sounds simple, but it's crucial. The average trader never defines his beliefs, and it crushes him. You can't have a clear strategy without clear beliefs. That leads into the next point: You must have a proven strategy that you believe in, and you must follow it to the letter.

Whether you're Ray Dalio, Warren Buffett, or Paul Tudor Jones, if you want to make money, you need beliefs that inspire a strategy, and then you need to vow to follow that strategy completely. The strategies vary, but the commitment to having and following them doesn't.

It took me years of failure and study to adopt these beliefs, but finally, they've become second nature. Pay close attention to the list below, and start to drill these beliefs into your head.

The Beliefs All Top Traders Share

Know your goals and objectives before you start trading, and before developing any strategy.

By knowing what outcome you're seeking beforehand, your strategy will take about 80 percent less time to create. When you don't have an objective or goal, you tend to tread water, because you can't make a plan without an endpoint. Set your objective, then make a plan to get there. You need to take a bit of extra time beforehand to save 80 percent of your time later and guarantee success.

The clearer your objectives, the easier the development process, and the easier the execution. Don't skimp on this.

Don't trade at all on days in which there are no low-risk trades available.

It's common to think you have to trade every day, but that leads to big losses on days when you shouldn't have traded at all. Don't be afraid to sit out a day. You should only be trading low-risk ideas that fit your strategy, and that has nothing to do with your calendar. A day without a trade isn't a lost day; it's a win, because you've avoided losses.

Good trading is boring.

The way to succeed in trading is to overcome all of your psychological weaknesses as a human. Those weaknesses can make life fun, but trading is about being rational, even robotic. The only reason I am so profitable is that I apply the rules of my trading strategy perfectly. That means following protocol 100 percent, which goes contrary to my earlier mistake of using trading as grounds for adventure. That was a recipe for disaster. Setting good rules and then following them to the letter is the only way to be profitable. To win the game, you have to follow all of the rules of the game, as boring as that may be. Break rules elsewhere.

That frustrated me at first, and I didn't want to execute the boring parts of trading (order management, setting and following rules and protocol). I wrote a complete script, hired an employee who enjoys executing rules to a tee, and trained him for two weeks. The process used to cost me many hours a week, but now it's outsourced to an employee who enjoys it. He sends me a report three times a day, which costs me a couple of minutes, total, to monitor. That saves me from boredom, and it allows me lots of time to research for more noncorrelated strategies and ways to improve the big-picture trading operation. That's my strength and what I enjoy.

When I finally mastered my psychological state, outsourced my weaknesses, and got disciplined, my accounts blossomed. I stopped thinking about the money as exciting *money*, but rather as boring transactions that I could measure objectively and precisely. I was finally able to trade comfortably at a risk profile that suited my needs. I stopped thinking about money gained and lost on a daily basis, because I knew that focusing on my proven rules would lead to *long-term* success, which is the true purpose of trading.

Daily results are irrelevant. All that matters are your long-term objectives. When that has been set correctly, your state of mind shouldn't change based on daily results.
That means no elation on good days, but no misery on bad days. My wife can no longer tell the difference between winning and losing days, because I've defined my risk and long-term objectives correctly. I can't fail, because short-term fluctuations are irrelevant. I don't freak out or get stressed.

I have many losing days each year, but this no longer bothers me. I consider the day a win if I followed my rules with 100 percent perfection. On that scorecard, I never fail. The daily losses are part of the game of getting rich long term. As Ray Dalio said in the book *The New Market Wizards*, "I'm not paid when I'm right 80% of the time. I only get paid when I make money." Daily wins and losses aren't real money made; they're just temporary, meaningless changes in the scorecard. Trading is a business, and the losses are expected business costs in a profitable endeavor. Would you question needing to pay rent for your jewelry store? Every business has necessary costs in order to achieve a profit at the end of the quarter, and trading is no different.

To be successful in trading, you need to lose to be able to win. Without risk, you can't win.

Entry size matters more than entry price.
The first time I read this was in Jack Schwager's book, *Hedge Fund Market Wizards*, and he is spot on. If you've sized your entrance correctly according to your risk tolerance, you'll stay with the position. You won't override it, because you've risked the proper amount of money, and you're OK with losing an exact, predetermined amount based on said risk tolerance. You aren't risking enough to affect your mental state so that you override your position.

On the other hand, when you've sized your entrance too high for your risk tolerance, you'll look at things differently when you start to lose money. If you bought a stock at 40 and the price drops to 39.50, you shouldn't be affected. However, if your entry was too big, you'll think in terms of dollars lost, and want to get out. Your exit won't be determined by price movement, as it should, but rather because of your dollar loss. Proper entry sizes will protect you from this.

Successful trading can be effortless, when you're committed and have worked hard up front.
Trading is easy for me, but only because I put in the preparation and years of practicing and commitment. I know every aspect of my trading strategies, so implementation is easy. I don't get tired or stressed anymore. You can do the same, if you work to get there.

Everyone has inborn personality weaknesses for trading, but as long as you account for yours, you'll succeed.

There are certain personality aspects, like patience and discipline, that are ideal for successful trading. But everyone has weaknesses, and you're only doomed to fail if you don't admit and account for your weaknesses.

The key is having the willingness to work on your weaknesses, so that you can transform them. Also, acknowledge them, so that they can be leveraged.

I personally hate discipline and rules, but I've committed myself to working on that weakness. You can do the same; it's your willingness to improve that matters most. I chose to work on myself, and now there is no doubt I will follow my rules, daily. That said, I've made my rules realistic, sacrificing some potential profits to ensure I follow my rules. Otherwise, I'd fail, and catastrophe would ensue.

It's just money. Be humble in victory.

You will see huge, daily profits at times. But remember: All that matters are long-term results. If you get cocky or greedy, the market will teach you a lesson.

*You **must** know your risk tolerance. It's lower than you think.*

If you try and guess your risk tolerance, you'll be wrong. You can't know until you've visualized losing money intensely, or ideally, actually lost money. That's how I learned. Now, it's a joy that I know my results can *never* affect my state of mind.

You won't lose a minute of sleep, even on your worst day of

the year, because you've defined your low limit precisely and have crafted your strategy so that you never exceed your risk tolerance. This means you sacrifice a small percentage in profits, long term, but it ensures you're 100 percent comfortable at all times. You'll never lose your cool and override the strategy, and you'll still make more than enough money, long term. Of course, the upside has to be there, too, but we ensure that when creating our strategies. It's not like you'll liquidate all positions at the slightest scare.

Virtually everyone overestimates their drawdown tolerance. Think you can handle a 30 percent drawdown? You'll almost certainly feel uncomfortable at 15 percent, losing sleep, wanting to override your strategy. That's normal. Don't set your risk tolerance until you've clearly visualized how such a change in your account balance will impact your psyche. And remember: The higher the drawdown, the harder it is to come back and break even. At a 30 percent drawdown, you need to make 43 percent to return to breakeven; but at a 50 percent drawdown, you'll need to make 100 percent. Ouch.

Project your strategy's results in all market types.
The main tenet of my strategies is that we don't try to predict which type of market is about to occur, because it's too difficult. We trade a set of noncorrelated strategies, so that we can make money in any type of market. You must know how your strategy works in each market type, so you're set for all possible scenarios.

Each strategy has times when it loses some money. That's common sense. A long-only strategy will struggle to make money during bear markets. As long as you knew this before-hand, you won't worry. You are ready for this and have other noncorrelated strategies in play that are making money. You will often have individual strategies losing, but the others will make up for them.

There is no Holy Grail strategy that works at all times.
I spent years searching for the perfect strategy. It stressed me out, and I lost years of trading because when I couldn't find the perfect strategy, I thought I was missing something. I beat myself up mentally and sat on the sidelines. Once I realized the perfect strategy doesn't exist, I was free to trade a *decent* strategy that makes money. The truth is, this strategy I thought was *decent* was about as good as it gets. All that matters are long-term profits.

The Holy Grail is in yourself. The Holy Grail is about conditioning your psychology and discipline and finding a strategy that suits your personality and objectives. You won't be right all of the time, but you will make more money than you need, long term. It's freeing to know that perfection is impossible, and "good enough" is truly more than you need.

The Holy Grail of stock trading is in the perfect execution of an automated suite of noncorrelated strategies, traded simultaneously.

Your strategy's back-tested success rate is *not* the same as its future success. Trust me, as all of my strategies are creat-ed through back testing. The best you can hope for is similar success, but you may have your worst drawdown ahead of you.

Your strategies must not only back test well, but they must be *conceptually correct*, otherwise you simply found something that was coincidentally lucky in the past and that is doomed to fail in the future.

Having the belief that you can't predict the markets is valuable and freeing, because it gives you the confidence to close a trade that has gone against you. You understand that short-term losses are inevitable, and you're OK with admitting you were "wrong," because you'll be right in the end.

Be wary of super-successful, back-tested strategies.
There might be a bug. You might have unconsciously overoptimized your strategy parameters. It might have been a coincidence. The key for all strategies, after development but before implementation, is to do everything possible to try and disprove your strategy. You must ensure that it's conceptually correct.

This is uncomfortable, because it goes against human nature to try and break your impressive creation. But in the end, you'll be grateful. I do this often with my business partner—when I've finished creating a new strategy, I send it to him and say, "Try and break it." I tell him to ensure that the great results from back testing were real, that the parameters weren't lucky, overoptimized, or due to huge data mining without conceptually correct ideas.

The future cannot be scripted perfectly from the past. Evaluate every parameter in your strategy. If you disprove a promising strategy, that can be frustrating, but it will save you a lot of money. Celebrate the fact that you avoided disaster.

A mistake isn't a losing trade. A mistake is failing to follow your rules.

Losing trades are part of the game. Don't consider them a failure. As long as you follow your rules 100 percent, you will succeed, because you have created the foundation for success beforehand. On the odd chance you overrode your strategy and it made you money short term, you should consider that a loss and a failure. You can get lucky short term, but the market will soon teach you a lesson.

Profitable trading can be simple.

I always used to think you needed to be a highly educated genius who knew every bit of financial news to be a successful trader. Most people think that. Once I realized that the news is all noise, and that your psychology is what determines results, my mind-set transformed.

A perfect example is the famous "turtle experiment." The strategy, created by Richard Dennis and Bill Eckhardt, was a simple breakout strategy with advanced position sizing. That was all. Yet the best-performing turtle achieved his results because he followed every rule. Some of the other turtles didn't follow their rules strictly, and their performance suffered. They were all using good strategies, but the winner was the one who followed his most closely.

The simplicity of a strategy, and its conceptual correctness, is what gives you your first edge. Then add proper, realistic objectives and a smart position-sizing strategy, and you're set if you follow the rules. It's not magic, just common sense.

Only trade strategies that fit your personality.
Long-term trend-following strategies work, and yet I don't trade them as a single strategy. I only trade them in combination with other strategies. I know myself, and I tend to be impatient with strategies like that. You have to be willing to give back a portion of your profits with long-term trend following, and that frustrates me. It works for other people, but I know it will affect my psychology and cause me to ignore the rules, so I simply forget about it.

Position sizing is key in helping you achieve your objectives.
The strategy isn't what makes you achieve your objective; position sizing does. I always thought that if I had a great strategy, I could make 100 percent a year. But it all depends on your drawdown tolerance, which determines your position sizing. If your drawdown tolerance is 10 percent per year, it will be hard to achieve a 100 percent yearly return. Your expected return (depending on your strategy) will be closer to 20 to 30 percent, at best. If you're willing to lose 50 percent, you can shoot for the moon and potentially achieve a 100 percent return.

It's important to know that your strategy *must have a statistical edge*. You cannot turn a negative expectancy strategy (one that doesn't make money in back tests) into a winning strategy by using a magic algorithm. That algorithm doesn't exist.

It's not about which particular stocks you buy; it's about your strategy, and your objectives, which define your position-sizing strategy and therefore your potential returns. Trading without a clear objective, as I did for years, is like driving with no direction, turning on whichever streets catch your eye. You won't get to your desired destination.

When in doubt, liquidate your position, or at least lower your exposure to the point that it doesn't influence you psychologically. All good trading books discuss this. You must have an objective view of the current market. When you're in the market, your brain tends to justify any type of market behavior, and all objectivity is gone. As soon as a position makes you anxious, get out. You can always get back in later.

Let's say you are long in a certain position. The market is going down, and you keep losing on that position. However, you're frustrated, and you have a big emotional charge on this position. No matter what happens, you'll defend it. You will find any reason why it's good to stay in the stock, because you want to be *right* and not admit defeat. Of course, this is *confirmation bias*—the mind just feeding you with the information you want to hear.

You must log all of your trades and mistakes.
I hate documenting my trades, but it's essential to be successful, because it gives you a wealth of insight. It tells you how your strategy is performing and the percentage of trading rules you're following. For discretionary traders, you can document your thoughts of each trade, then later identify winning and losing patterns to evaluate your decision making. I've logged my trades, with mistake logs, since 2009, and I discovered there was a bug in my software that overstated testing results. If I hadn't logged

my trades, that would still be affecting me.

You are not your thoughts.

This Buddhist sentiment might seem an odd inclusion for a trading book, but it's been one of my biggest insights. For years, I had limiting beliefs and low self-esteem, and this crushed my hopes at making money trading, not to mention my happiness.

The internal chatter in your head is holding you back from creating a profitable strategy. I was living my negative thoughts, yet totally unaware of it, and it hindered my performance in both trading and life.

Your thoughts are not reality; they're your perception of reality. For example, I used to think only a few people had the privilege to know the secret formula of the markets, so I could never be successful. But I realized I only thought that because of my past, failed experiences. My brain connected the dots incorrectly, saying that my past failures must have guaranteed future failure. But the truth was, I just had to change my beliefs to believe it was possible, then find a winning strategy.

Five years ago, I used to think all of my thoughts were true. I've since worked deeply on myself, and I've realized I was making everything up. My beliefs were all stories I told myself and accepted as true, even though they weren't. After deep practice, I am aware of any thought that isn't based on reality, so I can let it go. I no longer concern myself with what others think of me; they're just thoughts that don't affect who I am, as long as I'm being true to myself.

I'm happier, and I approach problems differently. Problems

used to consume me. Now, I know I cannot change external situations. I see everything as a minor issue, because blowing something up into a big issue does nothing to change the situation and everything to destroy my state of mind.

Know your strength and weaknesses.
I never knew who I was, so I didn't do anything with 100 percent commitment or conviction. I knew I had potential, and I knew it wasn't being used.

My journey of self-discovery and psychological transformation changed everything. I realized I no longer had to be the model corporate-type person to succeed—I could be myself. Those people had their strengths, but they also had their weaknesses, and I had my own unique strengths.

Now, I've accepted my weaknesses. I dislike working on details and have no programming skills nor the desire to learn. For that reason, I've hired a programmer to test my ideas. My biggest strength is creativity and the ability to create strategies, so I simply tell them to my programmer and double my leverage. I'm great at translating a complex, difficult world like trading into clear and simple-to-understand concepts.

I used to be full of trading ideas but never followed through on testing or implementing them. By accepting and outsourcing my weaknesses to someone for whom it's a strength, we both benefit, and I've succeeded with a more than 99 percent efficient application of my strategies. I've overridden my strategy on less than 1 percent of trades, and unsurprisingly, the profits have been massive.

Create Your Strategy

After you've understood these beliefs and how they relate to you, you can move on and create your strategy, which starts with defining your objectives. If you can define your objectives clearly, the development process of your strategy is actually quite simple, because you know exactly what you want it to achieve. Most people start with ideas, looking for strategies that work, but they don't know what they're looking for. You must start by defining your objectives, then moving on to identifying sound market principles.

In order to clarify your objectives, start by **defining your initial trading capital.** That's self-explanatory, of course: How much money are you willing and able to invest? But it's important to write it down, so that the other steps are done properly.

Based on that number, **what's the largest percentage drawdown you can withstand?** We define that number in percentage points, but you need to be aware of what that number will look like in terms of your trading balance—in dollars lost. It's easy to pick a number like 20 percent, but how many actual dollars is that, and are you sure you would be OK losing that much? I've met plenty of people with $1 million trading accounts who say a 20 percent drawdown is fine, then freak out when they've lost $200,000.

Then consider: **How long of a drawdown can you withstand? At what point will you stop trading and reevaluate? Do you differentiate between drawdown from base capital and profits drawdown?**

For both of these questions, visualize the loss in your account balance. Do you still want to trade your strategy, or are you anxious to get out? If your mental state will be affected, you need to set a more conservative number. The most obvious example was people who were trading buy and hold from 2005 to 2007 but who hadn't defined their drawdown threshold beforehand. Then 2008 came, and they didn't sell because they didn't know when to. So they hit 50 percent to 70 percent drawdowns, sold everything, and refused to trade ever again. They weren't basing their decisions on sound market principles but rather on just the temporary position of their equity.

Since that time, the market has tripled in value. If they had set their risk tolerance beforehand, they would have sold earlier, gotten back in the game, started to make money again in 2009, and profited ever since. Their buy-and-hold approach still worked, but they let their emotions override the strategy.

Don't think only in terms of percentages losses. Think also in concrete terms of *dollars lost*. You need to be in a mental state where losing money won't affect your decision making. Thinking in terms of percentages makes sense rationally, but humans are not rational when money is involved.

You need to trust in your strategy 100 percent, because you put in the work to perfect it beforehand. You need to know that short-term losses, even losing months of 5 to 10 percent, are part of the process. If you're down 5 percent, while your peers are making money, will you still follow your strategy?

A general rule I've found is that people can handle about half of what they think they can. If your instincts say you can handle a 20 percent drawdown, start with a 10 percent max drawdown to be safe, and learn from experience. It's far better to be safe than sorry, because overriding your strategy negates all of the work you did and destroys your finances.

If you have past trading experience and were comfortable losing a certain amount of money, start there.

By trading within your drawdown tolerance, you ensure that you'll stay comfortable and therefore rational.

I also recommend including a small margin of error in your strategy because you might make some trading mistakes and override your strategy occasionally. That's not ideal, but it's normal and not catastrophic if you've built in margin for error. If you set your compounded annual growth rate (CAGR) at 25 percent, are you OK with achieving 18 percent? And if your maximum drawdown is set at 7 percent, are you OK if it reaches 12 percent? Humans make mistakes, so make sure you're OK with slightly worse-than-expected results, compared to your back testing.

What is the CAGR you'll use in back tests? The larger drawdown you defined, the larger CAGR you can achieve. The more potential risk you can tolerate, the more potential reward you can reap. But it's important to define your risk first, otherwise you'll shoot too high. It's better to be safe than sorry. If you need to be conservative with your risk, that's fine, but don't expect huge returns. Lots of potential clients tell me they won't tolerate a drawdown beyond 10 percent, but they want a CAGR of 100 percent per year. I tell them that's not possible and to ignore anyone who tells you it is. You might get lucky for one or two years, but not long term. If you're testing a maximum 10 percent drawdown, aim for a CAGR of around 20 to 30 percent. The longer you trade, the more you will realize that even the best strategies *will* have a larger than expected drawdown. Prepare for that beforehand.

Will you trade on margin? You need to define if you will only trade the amount of equity you have, or if you are willing to go over that, *on margin*. For example, you can trade 150 percent of your account value, if 100 percent is long and 50 percent is short. That's allowed, because your exposure is only 50 percent net long. The short positions are allowed to offset the long positions. However, are you comfortable trading on margin? Also, if you trade IRA accounts, know that you can't trade on margin.

How will you handle larger-than-expected profits? This would be a good problem to have, but you still need to consider it. Let's say you're trading a long strategy on volatile stocks, and you've tested a return of 25 percent per year. In your first year, you see a return of 120 percent, because of something like the dot-com boom. It's important to answer beforehand: Will you want to withdraw capital? If so, you need a strategy in place that accounts for specific profit targets at which you will withdraw a specific amount of money. Otherwise, you'll withdraw money and it won't be accounted for in your strategy, and you're in trouble. Many people can't handle unexpected success. It's also important to consider this on an individual scale. How will you react if you earn a 150 percent profit on one positon? If you're going to feel compelled to withdraw money, you need to account for that. It's fairly easy to design a position-sizing algorithm to help you with such a problem. Make sure that greed isn't ruining your strategy.

Everyone thinks this is a no-brainer, but greed *always* kicks in.

Will you use a benchmark? If so, which one, and why? In my strategies, the benchmark isn't important. A benchmark is a long-only performance of an index. We trade a suite of non-correlated strategies, so we don't really care what the benchmark does; we do our own, separate, noncorrelated thing. But the whole world and media is obsessed with benchmarks: *What did the S&P do today?* It's important to think about how you will react if, for example, your strategy earns you 10 percent one year, but the index is up 40 percent and everyone around you is bragging about their long-only strategies. That could influence your mental state. It's important to know how you'll react to the news.

Intellectually, it's easier to understand that a benchmark is not useful for trading. As we've shown, the benchmarks don't perform particularly well, and they have seen huge drawdowns. They're simple and easy to beat, so you shouldn't look at them, because outside noise *will* influence you.

That said, reality sometimes interferes with this. Not everyone can ignore the news. Let's say you're trading a noncorrelated strategy of long-term trend following, mean reversion, and other strategies together. Suddenly, there's a bull market like the 1999–2000 dot-com boom. All you'll hear on TV and at parties is how easy it is to make money in the stock market. They're handing out 60 to 70 percent returns, every year! Your friends are bragging, nonstop.

Short-term, this is easy to deal with. But what if there are two or three years of outside noise? What if your spouse starts to ask, "Why is everyone making more money than us?" She doesn't think you're doing a good job, and you can't blame her—all of her colleagues and friends are bragging, too.

You know that there will be a turnaround—that the people creating noise will lose their money, *eventually*. But as we've drilled in—there's no way to predict when the markets will turn. Are you patient enough to wait a couple of years? The years of noise could get to you.

If you think there is a high likelihood of your hearing outside noise—from your friends, colleagues, spouse, or the media—consider the benchmark. Don't be a slave to it, but consider it. Make sure that you will make outsized gains in bull markets, because otherwise, you may struggle to follow your strategy.

The benchmark is only relevant in bull markets. In all other markets, you'll be positive, while others are losing. As long as part of your strategy is long-term trend-following positions with volatile stocks, you should be prepared.

As you'll see in part 4, the first strategy—the "Weekly Rotation strategy"—is perfect for this.

How will you react when you're underperforming the benchmark by a little? A lot? Will you accept years when you underperform the benchmark? I don't compare my results to the benchmark, but some people like to. That's fine, but make sure you have a strategy for when the benchmark outperforms you. Be aware that this *will* happen occasionally, but it shouldn't bother you. When the markets are up huge, yes, the benchmark will beat you. But when the markets are down, you'll be losing less than the markets. Long term, you'll be making much more money than someone who follows the benchmark.

Are you OK with cutting losses short and riding profits out? With trend following especially, people have a tendency to take profits and let losses run. It's a normal, cognitive bias, but you need to be aware of it and not fall prey. People want to feel good about themselves, so they take a profit. Feeling good about yourself has nothing to do with good trading, though, and nor does taking a profit when you could have made more.

It's common for people to want to take a profit 80 percent of the time, but those profits will be small. Winning 80 percent of the time means you'll lose 20 percent of the time, and people who behave like this will be unable to cut those losses short. The 80 percent of wins could be, say, $10 each, but the 20 percent of losses will run and could be $200 each. Despite "winning" 80 percent of trades, you would have lost a lot of money.

Winning trading isn't about winning more frequently; it's about your overall balance. You'll end up bankrupt if all you care about is taking profits, especially if you can't accept losses. We've been trained since youth to see losing as *wrong*. We've been trained to never admit defeat, or that we were wrong.

When we went to school as kids, we were graded for every exam—if you get A's or B's you're "good," and if you don't, you're "bad." "Bad" students are forced to think that *they can't make mistakes*, and they're often stuck with this mentality for life. Well-meaning parents raise their kids to be afraid of making mistakes, by teaching *right versus wrong*. Even though I'm aware of this, I've done it with my own kids, accidentally. It's unfortunate, but it's reality.

The belief that you *don't make mistakes*, because you're perfect, or you *can't make mistakes*, because then you're "bad," is trading suicide. A strategy that is only "right" 30 percent of the time can be the perfect strategy, if your winners are five times larger than your losers.

Intellectually, this is easy to understand, yet people still fall prey to these biases. Just because you *know* something doesn't mean you'll execute it when your psychology and emotions come into play. You need to understand deeply that wins and losses aren't measured by individual trades; they're measured by how perfectly you're executing your strategy. It's not the profits on a single trade that will make you rich. It's the net balance of all of your wins and losses, and how big each one is. Keep your losses as small as possible, and maximize your wins. Your strategy will take care of this, if you follow it.

Success has one definition: How closely are you executing your strategy, and trading within your risk tolerance? That's the only way you can grade yourself.

CHAPTER 7

The Secret Twelve-Ingredient Recipe

When creating your own personal strategy, be aware that every trading strategy is different (long, short, combined, etc.) but has the same twelve ingredients. Even fundamental traders, which I don't work with, should use these same twelve steps. The better you can define these twelve steps, the easier it will be for you to understand every part of your strategy and therefore execute it.

In part 4, we'll go through each strategy I teach, specifically. For now, I'll give a brief overview of each of the twelve universal ingredients.

1. Objectives

We've discussed personal objectives (how much money do you expect to earn, long term?), but not the objectives of your strategy. Both are important.

Let's say you're going to trade a long-term, trend-following strategy. You want to always be positioned in the high-flying, uptrend stocks, capturing as much of the move as possible with particular trends. Therefore, your top objective is to ensure you're making a huge amount of money when the market is going up. You need the opposite objective, too, to be realistic: You will get out as your strategy has determined the trend is over. That's how you execute a trend-following strategy, by defining how to maximize wins, while accepting losses and cutting them as short as possible.

Before you test, and eventually trade, a strategy, you need well-defined objectives of what you hope to achieve. In order to trade a strategy successfully, it needs to be built on your beliefs, which work toward your objectives.

There are four types of objectives you must define: psychological, operational, personal, and strategy. Strategy objectives can be split up into single (for one strategy) and multiple (for a suite of strategies trading simultaneously).

Psychological objectives are set so that trading your strategy never affects your mental state. That involves setting your maximum drawdown, CAGR, trade frequency, if you will take any profits out of your strategy, and if you care about having a high win ratio, versus a high win-loss ratio. The higher win ratio you need, the better off you'd be using a mean reversion strategy with a profit target. A high win-loss ratio would mean the average winning trade is larger than the average loser, which would mean you should use a trend-following strategy.

Basically, if you prefer more wins of smaller magnitudes, you'll prefer a high win ratio (mean reversion with profit target).

If you prefer fewer wins of larger magnitudes, you'll prefer a high win-loss ratio (trend following).

Operational objectives are set to ensure you can operate your strategy stress-free, in a way that suits your lifestyle. Will you enter trades weekly, or daily? Some people like to do it intraday. Do you want to enter the trades yourself, automate them, semi-automate them, or hire someone?

Personal objectives are important, too. Will your spouse, children, or other family members influence your trading strategy? Does your spouse work at an investment bank, where he or she can't ignore benchmarks? That could cause problems in years where there are big bull markets.

Next, strategy objectives. If you're going to trade multiple strategies, what are the single objectives for that strategy? What does it do? How does it react in bull markets? What about bear markets, sideways markets, volatile markets, quiet markets, and normal markets? What about different combinations of those? You need to plan for every possible scenario. Once you start combining strategies, you have to make sure your strategies work well with each other. If you have a long-term, trend-following strategy and then develop a short strategy, does one make money when the other doesn't?

When trading multiple strategies, it's important that they're designed to help each other. They're like partners, complementing each other's weaknesses.

All of my students who fail to define their objectives struggle to create a strategy. Once you do, you simply use the indicators to measure price action, define your rules, and get going.

Most people want the highest possible return with the lowest drawdown and think that is their main objective. That leads to the creation of strategies that don't suit their psychology or objectives. They self-sabotage themselves to bankruptcy.

2. Beliefs

Your objectives are linked to your beliefs. For example, trend following is a sound belief that the markets are mostly trading sideways. However, when they trend, you can make huge money if you capture the trend. Your objective could be to capture just 25 percent of the moves, because profits are so big. You'll need a profit target in your objectives, so your indicators and rules can tell you what to do. Another belief could be to buy fear when everyone is panicking, because there's a larger than normal likelihood that the market will revert back to its mean. Those are two core, simple, yet effective and proven beliefs. For every strategy, you need to understand the underlying core belief and market principle. If you aren't clear on the belief you're trading, you'll lose confidence and fail to execute.

It's essential to test your beliefs and make sure they're based on sound market principles.

You're not trading the markets; you're trading your beliefs. Inside the stock market, you've got hundreds of thousands of people, each with their own opinions. Maybe 5 percent of them really make money, but 100 percent of them have beliefs about where the market will go. In order to make money, you need to hypothesize beliefs, back test them to see if they're true, and if they are, develop a strategy based on those beliefs. The market does what it does. It doesn't care what you think. You can only trade according to your beliefs, and you'll only make money long term if your beliefs are scientifically and logically true.

Often you'll start with a belief, back test it, realize it doesn't work, but in the process, see something else that works. For example, you might start with the beliefs that buying the highest high of the last twenty days has an edge, because the Turtles Group used to trade that entry signal. The Turtles Group had been extremely successful in the futures market in the 1980s, and that belief seems sound. But if you back test, you will see that while it made huge money in the 1980s, it has mainly been flat, with some huge drawdowns, ever since. However, you'll see that a larger timeframe like one hundred or two hundred days actually works, so you can shift to that belief.

By documenting and tracking your trades, you'll develop new beliefs and get stronger evaluations of your current ones. At least once a year, you should reevaluate your beliefs and make sure they are all still sound—that nothing has changed. That doesn't mean you should change parameters frequently, but you should monitor things occasionally. If you start seeing statistically larger-than-expected downturns, you may need to scrap and redefine your beliefs.

3. Trading Universe

Are your objectives and beliefs clear? Move on. What are you going to trade? This book only addresses stocks, but of course there are other instruments you can trade. In the United States, we have over seven thousand listed stocks. What's your trading universe? Do you want to trade the complete basket of NYSE, American Exchange, and NASDAQ stocks? Do you want to trade an index like the S&P 500 or NASDAQ 100? They all have their pros and cons.

If you want to trade a high-frequency strategy, it might be easier to have a large portfolio. Therefore, you'll need a larger universe to trade within. The same goes for mean reversion; since your expected profit per trade is low; you capture a short profit, get out, and repeat frequently. You make numerous, frequent trades—trading mean reversion on a small index like the Dow Jones can result in some great trades, but you won't have enough opportunities to make a significant profit. Generally, the larger the universe, the more trade opportunities. You need a ton of opportunities for mean reversion to be worth trading. Twenty trades a year will not do enough for your finances, regardless of how many of them are winners.

If you want to trade a long-only strategy, you're basing it on the belief that since indexes rebalance every three months, the weaker companies are kicked out. That might be information that would benefit you when developing a trend-following strategy. Trend following is the opposite of mean reversion, because you'll stay in one position for a long time, but capture a big profit.

On the other hand, it's OK to use trend following on a very large portfolio, with strict selection filters. You can trade trend following on the complete stock universe, but you need more filters to get the stocks you really want.

That's why I recommend adopting the belief that you need an index, even though there is nothing wrong with including stocks not yet in an index. Microsoft, for example, was a tiny stock when it started—not yet it an index. Therefore, it's fine to include early stage stocks in addition.

4. Filters

You need a filter for liquidity, to ensure there's enough volume to buy the stocks your strategy dictates. It depends on your account volume, though. If you have a $50,000 account, you can trade fairly low-volume stocks (average trading volume of ~100,000 shares). If you have a larger account, you can't trade those stocks. You would move the market too much with each trade. One idea is to set your volume filters based on your account size. Another one is to make sure you have a filter to never trade more than a small percentage of the average dollar volume. For shorting, volume is even more important, because you need decent liquidity—you need to have some shares that are available to short.

If you have a lower account, you actually have an advantage, because you have access to stocks that the big players don't have access to. That is a *huge* edge. Use it if you can.

You also need a minimum price filter. Some people don't like penny stocks, so they'll need to set a higher minimum price.

Lower-priced stocks move differently than stocks trading at, say, thirty cents. If you trade a stock that is priced at eighty cents, expect crazy moves and volatility.

You need a volatility filter. I think it's smart to filter out stocks at the extreme ends of both high and low volatility. That's a controversial belief, because some people think that using volatility-based position sizing is enough. I think you need some filters, because if you're selecting a stock that has an average volatility that's twenty-times less than the S&P 500, it will not move at all and won't help you. Trading on the higher end is possible, but it provides us with margin issues. Setting volatility filters beforehand is safe. Based on your beliefs and objectives, you'll decide what kind of volatility you want in your portfolio.

5. Setup

You need to define the exact rules of what the movement of a particular stock should look like before you enter a trade. We only use end-of-day price action data, so we ask: Which numbers will fulfill our rules that tell us which stocks to buy or short the following day? An example setup could be to buy a trend that is closing above the two-hundred-daily moving average—or short sell a stock that is highly overbought. A setup can define a trend, a pullback, or anything else, as long as it defines a clear situation that fulfills a set of criteria that tells you what to buy or short sell the following day.

If you have clear beliefs and objectives about what kind of entry you're looking for, then you just use a technical indicator that does what you want. If you know what your entry needs to look like—say, your objective is to enter a trending stock—use a technical indicator (moving average, highest high, etc.) to quantify your belief and objective.

For example, if your belief/objective is to find stocks that are oversold, because they'll revert back to their mean, you need an indicator that measures that. You could use the Relative Strength

Index (RSI), buying when it dips below a certain threshold.

Define your beliefs and objectives first, then look for indicators that help quantify them.

6. Ranking

There will be times that your strategy generates more setups (suggested trades) than your position sizing allows. It could tell you to make fifty trades one day, but your position sizing (risk management) only allows ten. You decide which ten to trade based on your ranking parameters.

It depends on your strategy and preferences, but you could trade the ten stocks with the highest volatility, lowest volatility, largest rate of change, the most oversold, or perhaps the strongest short-term trends.

For a mean reversion example where you buy pullbacks, you could say you want the ten pullbacks with the most volatile movements, or the most oversold, but those are different things. It can make a big impact on what you trade, so you need to define this beforehand.

7. Entry

Next, define your entry for situations in which the setup requirements have been fulfilled and you need to place an order. How are you going to enter the stock the next day? Will it be when the markets open, or does it need to advance for a certain amount, like a percentage or average true range? Or does it need to drop even further down? Is it a limit order? Is it a market order? Define this beforehand.

In part 4, I'll show you specific rules for each strategy, which should clarify these generalizations.

8. Stop Loss

When entering a position, you must have a predefined exit point, in order to limit your risk. This ensures that you don't stick with your losers if a trade doesn't work out as planned. You acknowledge your losers and sell them, taking your losses humbly, and moving on. That's a long-term win, despite feeling like a loss.

9. Reentry

After you get stopped out and sell a stock, will you reenter the stock immediately if it gives another signal? Or will you decide to hold off for a certain amount of time? It depends on the strategy. You could get the signal the day after you sold, which makes people uncomfortable. If you won't want to buy a stock you lost on, you had better put a rule in there. If there is a statistical edge to reenter, which is something you should have tested, you must obey your strategy and buy anyway.

10. Profit Protection

If you're in a trade that becomes profitable, will you have a set point in which you'll protect your profit? You can do this via a trailing stop, which will sell the stock when it loses more than X percent from its highest point. The trailing stop will move as the stock price rises. It's a way to protect your profits if a stock suddenly drops down.

11. Profit Taking

People who can't escape their ego and need to feel good about having as many "wins" as possible should set a profit target. You can say beforehand, for example, "When the stock achieves a 20 percent win, I'm getting out." It depends on your beliefs, objectives, and personality, but if you define it beforehand, it's fine. There are great strategies like this—they of course have smaller profits per trade, but they have higher win rates.

12. Position Sizing

Position sizing is what determines how much you are going to invest. Which strategy or mathematical algorithm and rules are you going to use to define the sizes of your positions that you trade? This is essential, so that you achieve your predefined objectives. I'll explain them in part 4, but the various strategies define your optimal risk. Proper position sizing is crucial, to ensure you make the most of your proven rules.

In the following part, we're going to show a variety of different strategies—each with different beliefs and objectives, suited for a variety of people. All of them have great edges and have been tested over a long period of time; the one you'll use simply depends on what you want—the one that most suits you.

Then, we'll show you how to combine the individual strategies into a suite of noncorrelated strategy, which multiplies your edge exponentially. That's because the strategies all perform differently in different market types, and as you know, the markets are crazy and unpredictable.

It's much easier than you think, and all of the strategies use simple, straightforward rules. Each one is an example of a strategy I've built, or helped clients build in my Elite Mentoring program, through my Trading Mastery School.

PART 4

Meet the Proven Strategies

CHAPTER 8

Weekly Rotation S&P 500— For the Busy or Lazy

Are you too busy to enter and exit trades during the week? The Weekly Rotation strategy only requires you to enter trades on weekends.

Or maybe you just have better things to do, or you're lazy. That's not a problem, as long as you account for it up front. If once-a-week trading fits your lifestyle best, or you don't want to be involved in the markets on a daily basis, this is the strategy for you.

It's also great for people with IRA or 401K accounts, because they can trade long only—and this strategy is long only.

If you listen to or watch the news, or are exposed to a lot of outside noise through work or social settings, this strategy will help. You'll mainly be in high-flying stocks like Netflix and Tesla—strong companies that attract positive media coverage.

It's a simple strategy that anyone can follow.

Objectives

- Trade long only, a big index, mainly blue-chip stocks that rise in value.
- Only execute trades *once a week* (during the week you don't need to check the markets at all).
- Jump on the train of big trending stocks, with the expectation that they will continue to rise.
- Strongly outperform the S&P 500 (at least double the CAGR), with lower drawdowns in bear markets.

Beliefs

Markets trade sideways, and they trend. My belief is that if we jump on the strongest performing stocks, we will have outsized returns trading them. We will stay in those positions as long as they continue to be the strongest performers in the markets. History has shown us over and over again that stocks can trend for a long time. Perfect examples are Microsoft, Apple, Dell, Netflix, and so on.

The biggest edge in this strategy is the unexpected, outsized, favorable returns.

As long as the trend is up and the stock is within the best ten performers of the universe, we remain in those stocks. Why would we sell a winning stock?

Trading Universe

- Only trade stocks from the S&P 500 index.
- For testing, this means we take into account all listed and delisted S&P 500 stocks, and their joiners and leavers data.

Filters

- Minimum Average Volume of the last twenty days is above 1,000,000 shares (so that we have enough liquidity).
- Minimum price is 1 USD.

Position Sizing

- We trade a maximum of ten positions, and we divide our equity by ten to calculate our position size. This is a very simple position-sizing strategy. Of course, depending on your objectives, we can trade the same strategy using a different algorithm.
- Example:
  - Total equity: 100,000 USD
  - Size per position: 100,000 / 10 = 10,000 USD
  - If stock price is trading at 40.00, we buy: 10,000 / 40.00 = 250 shares.

Entry Rules

1. Today is the last trading day of the week (typically a Friday afternoon or evening, after the market has closed). We take end-of-day data.

2. The close of the SPY (exchange-traded fund, or ETF, of S&P 500 index) is above the two-hundred-daily simple moving average (SMA) band.
   - There is a band set at 2 percent below the two-hundred-daily SMA.
     - The price can go below the two-hundred-daily SMA, but not by more than 2 percent.

- The two-hundred-daily SMA is a powerful and simple tool. Many institutional traders look at this moving average, but there is some noise involved. Many times the SPY closes below this average, only to go up again the following day, so we include a 2 percent buffer.
- As long as the stock is above the two-hundred-daily SMA band, we are allowed to enter positions.

   The SPY tracks completely the price of the S&P 500.

3. We trade up to a maximum of ten positions, and we select them as follows:
   - The three-day RSI (Relative Strength Index) of the stock is below 50.
     - RSI is an oscillator that measures how overbought or oversold a stock is. The higher the RSI, the more overbought the stock is.
     - Our method ensures the stock isn't completely overbought. We like to enter trending stocks, but the statistical edge diminishes if they are in extremely overbought conditions.

4. If rules 1–3 are true, then we select the ten stocks with the highest rate of change (ROC—percentage increase) over the last two hundred trading days.
   - We want to be in the biggest-moving stocks.
     - We're measuring momentum.

5. We enter the first day of the next week: market on open.

Exit Rules

1. Today is the last trading day of the week.

2. We stay in the same position as long as the stock is in the top ten of highest ROC over the last two hundred days. This means the stock is still on an uptrend. There is no reason to sell it.

3. We rotate into a new position as soon as the stock is not in the top ten anymore. This means we sell market at open on the next trading day *and* we replace the stock with a new stock that is in the top ten of the highest ROC (percentage return) over the last two hundred days.

4. In this strategy there are no hard stop losses.

   The reason for this is because of the exit rotation character. Since we rotate and are only in the strongest-moving stocks, a stop loss is not helpful, nor necessary. Also, setting stop losses on a weekly basis doesn't make sense, and our objective is only to trade once a week.

   The testing results are almost identical with or without stops. That is because the stop is rarely reached—when the stock starts to lose value, it gets replaced automatically.

   If you feel uncomfortable trading without stops, and would like to better define your risk, just place a 20 percent stop loss, which equals 2 percent risk of your account (20% stop loss x 10% position).

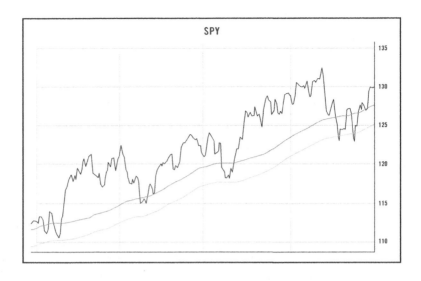

This is an example of the 200-SMA band. The dark grey line is the two-hundred-daily SMA, and the light grey line is the SMA band, which is 2 percent lower.

Ending Balance	5,041,642.28
CAGR%	19.61%
Max Total Equity DD	30.7%
Longest Drawdown	38.1
Wins	48.9%
Win/Loss Ratio	2.2
Average Days in Trade	35.84
R Squared	0.92
R Cubed	0.36
Annual Sortino Ratio	5.85
Ulcer Index	10.06

JAN 2, 1995 – NOV 23, 2016	TRADING SYSTEM	BENCHMARK
CAGR	19.61%	7.48%
Maximum Drawdown	30.67%	56.47%
Worst One Month Return	-13.82%	-16.52%
Worst One Day Return	-10.01%	-9.84%
Annualized Volatility	20.54%	19.31%
Sharpe	0.95	0.39
MAR	0.64	0.13
Daily Return Correlation to Benchmark	0.49	1.00
YTD Return	10.21%	8.26%
MTD Return	8.13%	3.83%
Total Return	**4,941.67%**	**385.05%**

For my testing, the software generated the following statistics: MAR, Sharpe ratio, R-squared, R-cubed, Sortino ratio, and Ulcer index. Each has its pros and cons. The most important thing is to clearly define your objectives before testing, so that you can identify which statistics will be most illustrative for your situation.

None of the statistics is a "magic number." There is no such thing as hitting a certain mark on one and being set for life. All of them are based on past data.

Institutional traders often use the MAR ratio and Sharpe ratio. The MAR (which stands for "Managed Accounts Report," the newsletter that developed this metric) is simply the relation between the CAGR and the maximum drawdown, a simple and clear g) ain-to-pain ratio. It's great to use, but it doesn't tell you anything about the duration of the drawdown. Also, once you've had a larger drawdown, the MAR will be punished for the duration of your time trading the strategy.

The Sharpe ratio is also used often by institutional traders—it's the most widely used method for calculating risk-adjusted returns. If you want to trade for institutions, a high Sharpe ratio will be useful to impress them. It measures the average period return, in excess of the risk-free rate, by the standard deviation of the return-generating process.

A variation of the Sharpe ratio is the Sortino ratio, which does not punish upside volatility and can be useful for trend-following strategies, where the edge lies in a small amount of outsized gains.

R-squared measures the slope of the equity curve, and R-cubed measures the relation of the CAGR, max drawdown, and the duration of the drawdown.

The Ulcer index measures the downside risk, and takes both the maximum drawdown and duration into account. The lower the Ulcer index, the better.

There is no magic indicator. Define your objectives and see which statistic or combination of statistics is most useful for you.

The benchmark is the S&P 500 in this example. As you can see in the back-tested results above, the CAGR is almost three times higher than the benchmark, the max drawdown is almost half, and the MAR (CAGR divided by maximum drawdown) is far superior. The Sharpe ratio is almost three times as good, and the strategy has a low correlation.

The win rate is not high, but a win/loss ratio of two to one means the average winning trade is twice the average losing trade. With trend following, that's your edge.

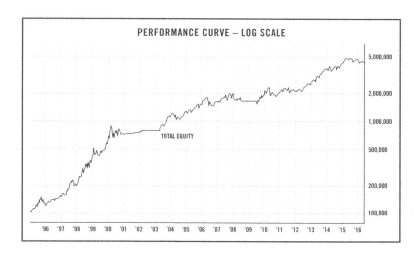

PERFORMANCE CURVE – LOG SCALE

TOTAL EQUITY

From 1997 to early 2000, there was a huge increase. Then, it was flat for two years. That's exactly the time where the S&P 500 dipped below the two-hundred-daily SMA band, meaning we stopped trading. During the bear market, we were flat. With the market going down, that's a great place to be.

After that, things kick off again, but go flat after the big bear market of 2008. By not doing anything with our money, we limit drawdowns, staying safe in cash. When the market recovered, we saw outsized returns.

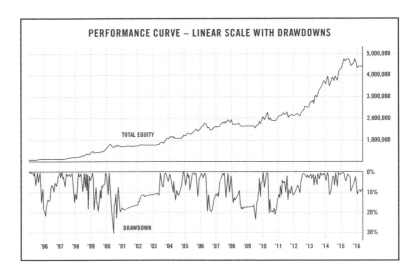

PERFORMANCE CURVE – LINEAR SCALE WITH DRAWDOWNS

TOTAL EQUITY

DRAWDOWN

It's crucial to understand that this strategy can be boring—in bear markets, you don't trade at all. That's a good thing—you're flat while others are losing.

The years 1998 and 1999 saw insane results, as you can see. Even in bear markets, we were still positive. Our benchmark here is the SPY, and as you can see, we outperformed it by a lot.

Basically, this strategy outperforms in bull markets, and it limits drawdowns—going flat—in bear markets. When the markets are going down, we don't have many trade setups. In sideways markets, it does OK—there isn't a clear up or down trend.

When you see huge, outsized returns one year, there may be a time when the market turns and you'll pay a price, with a big drawdown. That is to be expected when you're a trend follower.

As I've explained, you don't need to trade this strategy with stop losses. However, some people are so used to trading with stop losses that they feel uncomfortable when acting otherwise.

	JAN	FEB	MAR	APR	MAY	JUN	JUL	AUG	SEP	OCT	NOV	DEC	ANNUAL	SPY	COMPARISON
1995	2.09%	5.45%	2.26%	1.89%	2.15%	8.00%	7.08%	5.88%	1.90%	-3.00%	-6.51%	5.27%	22.81%	35.16%	-12.36%
1996	3.27%	3.27%	-0.31%	2.52%	3.94%	1.92%	-2.01%	3.42%	-0.13%	1.85%	4.21%	-0.07%	23.96%	20.31%	3.65%
1997	10.26%	-3.52%	-2.48%	6.58%	7.14%	0.42%	16.92%	-0.30%	6.38%	-10.49%	2.31%	-0.71%	34.12%	31.39%	2.73%
1998	7.85%	15.19%	-1.57%	10.97%	1.00%	8.27%	6.83%	-6.15%	18.56%	0.15%	-3.41%	14.14%	93.92%	27.04%	66.87%
1999	25.59%	-13.82%	6.71%	-4.27%	-2.51%	7.25%	1.68%	5.01%	-2.35%	7.42%	10.38%	23.08%	75.87%	19.11%	56.77%
2000	-5.15%	30.14%	-6.00%	-6.17%	-10.79%	11.43%	-5.21%	18.91%	-7.48%	-6.92%	-0.78%	1.21%	5.49%	-10.68%	16.17%
2001	-1.43%	0.41%	0.42%	0.40%	0.35%	0.31%	0.33%	0.31%	0.24%	0.20%	0.17%	2.58%	4.34%	-12.87%	17.21%
2002	2.56%	0.24%	0.52%	0.18%	-1.13%	0.17%	0.15%	0.14%	0.14%	0.14%	0.09%	0.10%	3.31%	-22.81%	26.12%
2003	0.09%	0.06%	-0.25%	6.50%	6.61%	-2.96%	0.46%	9.09%	3.86%	12.71%	2.24%	-0.56%	43.60%	26.12%	17.47%
2004	4.61%	0.16%	-3.61%	-8.12%	3.97%	1.52%	0.22%	-2.34%	2.04%	2.86%	9.59%	1.65%	12.09%	8.94%	3.15%
2005	-0.11%	5.06%	-2.45%	-5.18%	6.95%	1.39%	4.83%	4.80%	4.14%	-4.56%	2.40%	1.69%	19.29%	3.01%	16.28%
2006	11.92%	1.81%	6.78%	-2.14%	-6.66%	2.35%	-7.44%	-4.18%	-0.45%	7.58%	3.10%	0.54%	8.01%	13.74%	-5.74%
2007	0.81%	-3.85%	8.36%	1.84%	3.90%	-1.30%	2.45%	-1.77%	5.69%	0.73%	-3.50%	4.95%	19.02%	3.24%	15.78%
2008	-12.21%	1.04%	-1.31%	0.39%	1.62%	1.74%	-7.22%	0.42%	-0.63%	0.13%	0.03%	0.03%	-15.72%	-38.28%	22.56%
2009	0.01%	0.01%	0.01%	0.01%	0.01%	-1.07%	3.70%	1.98%	5.34%	-5.09%	6.45%	8.00%	20.33%	23.49%	-3.17%
2010	3.14%	4.04%	4.97%	-1.67%	-7.95%	-6.07%	0.53%	0.22%	0.26%	-0.65%	5.14%	1.45%	2.52%	12.84%	-10.32%
2011	3.14%	3.60%	5.09%	0.83%	0.57%	-2.08%	3.57%	-6.16%	-2.91%	2.79%	1.15%	-3.47%	4.39%	-0.20%	4.59%
2012	1.95%	2.95%	1.98%	-2.29%	1.66%	6.96%	-0.30%	3.04%	4.01%	2.12%	-0.16%	1.08%	21.80%	13.47%	8.33%
2013	-0.84%	-1.65%	5.08%	0.93%	6.34%	-2.27%	9.88%	-0.96%	6.10%	3.28%	4.19%	-0.35%	44.16%	29.69%	14.47%
2014	7.42%	5.93%	-6.47%	-2.31%	4.42%	4.86%	-4.55%	4.31%	0.85%	-1.32%	6.44%	1.10%	12.20%	11.29%	0.91%
2015	-0.71%	6.24	0.53%	-3.70%	6.01%	-2.14%	-0.63%	-4.12%	-0.79%	2.98%	2.91%	-1.46%	9.46%	-0.81%	10.28%
2016	-0.71%	6.24	1.48%	-2.25%	2.28%	2.51%	6.70%	0.31%	2.28%	-4.37%	8.13%		10.21%	8.26%	1.95%

The following chart explains how to trade the Weekly Rotation with stop losses.

We can clearly see that if we want to use a stop loss, small stop losses do not work well. That's because with these strong-moving stocks, we must allow them room. They are often quite volatile, so if we set small stop losses, they'll get stopped out. When we place the stop loss around 20 percent, the results are close to the original strategy's.

Now, we'll show some trade examples.

TEST STOP SIZE	CAGR%	MAR	MAX TOTAL EQUITY DD	LONGEST DRAWDOWN	WINS	WIN/LOSS RATIO
1%	9.55%	0.33	28.6%	85.0	14.8%	7.8
2%	11.36%	0.47	24.4%	48.8	21.1%	5.1
3%	12.20%	0.47	26.0%	47.9	26.7%	3.9
4%	13.32%	0.51	26.3%	48.5	31.1%	3.3
5%	13.50%	0.50	27.1%	83.6	34.9%	2.7
6%	14.22%	0.51	27.9%	83.7	38.5%	2.4
7%	14.90%	0.54	27.4%	38.2	40.5%	2.3
8%	15.20%	0.56	27.3%	38.6	42.3%	2.2
9%	15.34%	0.55	27.7%	39.0	43.5%	2.1
10%	15.45%	0.56	27.8%	38.8	44.9%	1.9
11%	15.22%	0.52	29.1%	45.2	45.2%	1.9
12%	16.11%	0.54	30.0%	38.8	46.0%	1.9
13%	15.96%	0.51	31.3%	39.0	46.3%	1.9
14%	16.18%	0.54	30.0%	39.1	47.3%	1.8
15%	16.39%	0.53	30.7%	38.9	47.5%	1.9
16%	16.64%	0.56	29.8%	38.9	47.7%	1.9
17%	17.17%	0.57	29.9%	38.9	48.3%	1.9
18%	17.04%	0.56	30.4%	39.2	48.2%	1.9
19%	17.39%	0.56	30.9%	39.2	48.9%	1.8
20%	17.75%	0.57	31.4%	40.0	48.9%	1.9
21%	17.84%	0.56	31.8%	40.0	49.2%	1.9
22%	17.81%	0.55	32.2%	41.9	49.2%	1.9
23%	17.78%	0.54	32.7%	41.9	49.3%	1.9
24%	17.88%	0.56	31.7%	40.0	49.1%	1.9
25%	17.91%	0.55	32.3%	42.0	49.2%	1.9
26%	17.83%	0.55	32.7%	42.3	49.2%	1.9
27%	17.87%	0.55	32.4%	42.3	49.1%	1.9
28%	17.82%	0.54	32.7%	42.4	49.4%	1.9
29%	18.11%	0.59	30.5%	39.1	49.2%	1.9
30%	18.10%	0.59	30.7%	39.2	49.4%	1.9

Example 1, Entry

After a long rise, DELL has entered the top ten stocks with the highest ROC over the last two hundred days, and it has an three-day RSI less than 50, so we enter on the open at the first day of the week.

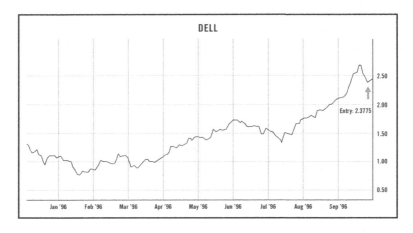

Example 2, Exit

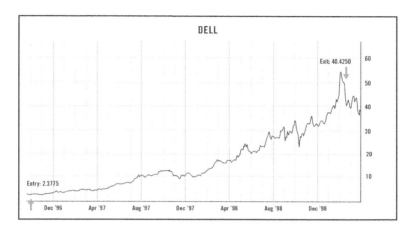

This was a dream trade, which we stayed in for over two years. The stock kept rising and was the whole time in its best performers.

Example 3

Entry: 85.04

Exit: 131.08

The Weekly Rotation strategy shows how easy it can be to make high double-digit returns, while working just thirty minutes a week. The simplicity of the strategy makes it easily tradable, yet you wind up with almost three times the annual return (19.7% CAGR) of the S&P 500, with almost half the drawdown.

You have one task each week. Check if the trend of the overall market is up, and if so, select the ten strongest-performing stocks (highest ROC) over the last two hundred days. Anyone can do it.

CHAPTER 9

Mean-Reversion Long—For Bold Contrarians

This strategy is great for people who like to be a bit more contrarian and who are comfortable trading against the herd. That means people who won't have trouble ignoring the news, and won't be susceptible to being affected by outside noise. Also, it is good for people with IRA accounts.

Objectives

- Trade long only on a large universe of stocks, taking advantage of oversold conditions by buying the best stocks and selling each when it reverts to its mean.
- Execute trade in less than thirty minutes a day.
- Take advantage of stocks that are in a long-term uptrend, that have significant volatility and are oversold on the shorter term. By buying these stocks even lower and selling them when they snap back, we have a consistent edge, and aim for 60 to 70 percent winning trades.

◻ Beat the overall market in both bull and sideways markets.

Beliefs

There are always times in which the markets will show such irrational, fear-based behavior that there is a statistically larger than normal probability that a reaction will cause a significant, opposite move.

Markets are driven by fear and greed. If we want to take advantage of this on the long side, we need to look for candidates that have shown a lot of fear. These stocks are mostly out of favor and have shown large sell-offs, mostly accompanied with larger than normal volatility.

There will come a time when the panic selling of these stocks will stop, and often this is when professional traders jump in and look for bargains. Statistically, there is an edge in "buying fear" and selling it when it has reverted, or shown some upward movement.

This kind of trading goes against human nature; it is trading against the herd. It is not easy to be a buyer when everybody is selling and all news messages show panic, but that is exactly what makes it a profitable strategy.

Since we are looking for a shorter-term trade (a couple of days), we need a large trade frequency. This is done by both scanning over a large stock universe, and creating exit rules so that we get out quickly.

Trading Universe

- We trade all US stocks from AMEX, NASDAQ, and NYSE (around seven thousand listed stocks).
- We trade a large basket of stocks, because we want a high number of trades (mean reversion trades are short term—therefore we need a high number of trades for significant profit).
- We do not trade ETFs, pink sheets, or bulletin board stocks.
- For testing, this means that we take into account all listed and delisted stocks. Since 1995, this list consists of around forty thousand stocks.

Filters

- Minimum Average Volume of the last fifty days is above 500,000 shares.
- Minimum price is 1 USD.
- Dollar volume is at least 2,500,000 USD.
  - This is to make sure that, if we're trading low-priced stocks, there's enough dollar volume for it to be worth trading.

Position Sizing

- - Fixed fractional risk: 2 percent
  - This means we take into account the dollar volatility of the stock.
    - ▷ The higher the volatility of the share prices, the lower our position will be, and vice versa.
- We trade a maximum of ten positions in this strategy.

- Each position risks 2 percent of our equity. The calculation of this is as follows.
  - Equity: 100,000 USD
  - Risk per trade: 2 percent
  - Dollar risk per position: 2,000 USD (2% x 100,000)
  - The risk is calculated by the difference between the entry price and stop loss price.
  - If the entry is at 20.00 USD and our stop loss is 17.00 USD, then we have a dollar risk per share of 3.00 USD.
  - How we calculate our desired position:
    - If we are risking a total of 2,000 USD per position, and this equals 3 USD per share, our size is: 2,000 USD / 3 USD = 666 shares.

We use this type of position sizing so that we know exactly what percentage of our equity we can lose on each position. Also, we define risk by the difference between the entry and stop loss. Since we use a wide stop loss, few trades get stopped out. If we close a position with a loss, we typically lose less than the total amount risked.

However, we have not yet defined our total size, just our risk per trade. There could be a time where a position gaps against us. In the previous example, we entered at 20.00 USD, and our stop loss was set at 17.00 USD, but there's a chance that an overnight news event could cause the stock to open at 10.00 USD. If that happens, our stop is irrelevant; we will suffer a large loss at the open price of 10.00 USD.

Also, in times of low volatility, the stop can limit us, because the stop is set based on the volatility. The lower the volatility,

- It's important to rank them, because we are only trading the ten *most-oversold* stocks. Without rankings, we could have fifty to two hundred setups to choose from.
- In this rule, we ensure that we're selecting the stocks which have the most fear.

7. The following day, before the market opens, we place a limit order of 4 percent below the current day's close.
   - That is because if there is intraday movement in which the stock moves further down, that simply means there is *more fear*.
   - That makes our trade stronger, because fear is good. We want fear in our stocks. There is a significant edge if we buy lower than we could have at the beginning of the day.

8. At the end of the day, we look at which orders were filled.

9. If we wanted to use a stop loss on the first day, we would need to watch the market the whole day in order to place a stop. Since we only want to work thirty minutes a day, we don't place stops on the first day. We could, but it's too much work and doesn't fit with our objectives. It also would make virtually no difference on your bottom line.
   - Test results are similar whether or not we use stops on the first day, as shown in the examples.

Exit Rules

1. When an order gets filled, we place a stop loss after that day's close. The stop loss is 2.5- times the ten-day ATR. That's wide, because we need to give the trades room. We are buying falling stocks, and for mean reversion, these stocks need space to develop.

   ◻ It's important to know that these trades must have a large stop loss. If we trade with small stops, this strategy doesn't work. The trade needs room to develop.

   ▪ This can be difficult on a psychological basis, because many positions will first show a loss after entry.

2. We stay in the trade until any of the following conditions is met:

   a. Stop Loss: The trade gets stopped out.

   b. Profit Target: When the position has earned a profit of 3 percent or more, we exit the following day, market on open.

   c. Time Exit: When four days have passed without A or B occurring, we exit market on close.

Ending Balance	7,657,816.66
CAGR%	21.92%
Max Total Equity DD	19.9%
Longest Drawdown	13.6
Wins	69.6%
Win/Loss Ratio	0.7
Average Days in Trade	2.52
R Squared	0.96
R Cubed	2.59
Ulcer Index	2.89

JAN 2, 1995 – NOV 23, 2016	TRADING SYSTEM	BENCHMARK
CAGR	21.92%	7.48%
Maximum Drawdown	19.93%	56.47%
Worst One Month Return	-8.52%	-16.52%
Worst One Day Return	-6.29%	-9.84%
Annualized Volatility	10.08%	19.31%
Average Exposure	10.35%	100.00%
Sharpe	2.18	0.39
MAR	1.10	0.13
Daily Return Correlation to Benchmark	0.31	1.00
YTD Return	19.92%	8.26%
MTD Return	5.08%	3.83%
Total Return	7557.82%	385.05%

Here's an explanation of the statistics used in the previous chart. R-squared measures the slope of the equity curve—it goes from 0 to 1, so 0.96 is excellent.

R-cubed is a measure of the relationship between the CAGR, the maximum drawdown, and its duration. The higher the measure, the better.

The Ulcer index measures how many ulcers you might get while trading—clearly, the lower the index, the better. In the world of trading, a 2.92 ulcer index is very low. It factors in the size and duration of drawdowns.

As you can see, this strategy has a great CAGR, reasonable drawdown—but contrary to the Weekly Rotation strategy, our win rate is extremely high. This is great for people who struggle to handle losses and don't like strategies with low win rates. The reason for this is because we have a very short-term profit target of 3 percent. Many trades reach that 3 percent and are exited with a profit. Mean reversion strategies are good for people who want higher win rates.

Also, the average exposure of 10 percent is very low. You may be 100 percent invested at times, but overall, your equity will be unexposed. We only trade when the time is right.

This strategy destroys the benchmark in all aspects, without correlating to it, as you can see.

The strategy would have turned $100,000 into more than $7 million, if you had traded it since 1995.

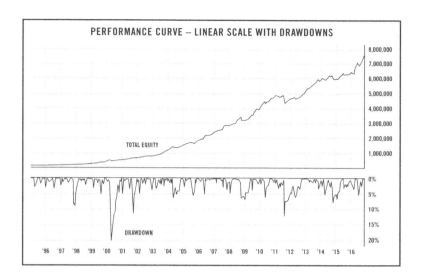

This chart shows the equity curve, juxtaposed with drawdowns. With this strategy, it's normal to be in drawdowns, but your winnings make up for it.

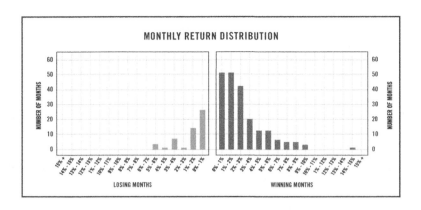

MONTHLY RETURN DISTRIBUTION

Before the largest drawdown, in 2000, there were significant gains. The drawdown occurred *because* of large accrued profits. Therefore, it's easier to stomach. It's expected.

The one negative year was very small. With mean reversion, the more volatility, the more trades we get. The mediocre years are a result of low volatility.

As you can see, there are far more dark grey months (making money) than light grey ones (losing money).

Performance has been mediocre in the last few years, but that is simply due to low volatility. In 2016, performance has picked up.

With mean reversion, the more volatility, the more trades we get. If there isn't a lot of volatility in the markets, we don't see a lot of setups, and our trade frequency is too low. I'm certain that as soon as the volatility picks back up, this strategy will perform exceptionally, as it has in previous high-volatility environments.

	JAN	FEB	MAR	APR	MAY	JUN	JUL	AUG	SEP	OCT	NOV	DEC	ANNUAL	SPY	COMPARISON
1995	1.10%	0.74%	-0.26%	-0.86%	1.42%	2.37%	2.05%	-0.37%	2.80%	7.05%	1.68%	0.91%	20.06%	35.16%	-15.11%
1996	0.61%	1.93%	-0.12%	-0.15%	-0.07%	10.27%	1.00%	1.72%	1.30%	1.94%	0.92%	1.70%	22.71%	20.31%	2.40%
1997	0.66%	1.61%	1.51%	0.85%	1.89%	-0.58%	1.50%	2.00%	3.68%	-5.11%	0.67%	3.53%	12.61%	31.39%	-18.78%
1998	2.39%	1.67%	2.36%	3.88%	1.61%	1.59%	0.73%	1.05%	2.32%	1.35%	1.65%	8.54%	33.06%	27.04%	6.01%
1999	7.91%	2.15%	9.33%	7.27%	4.43%	4.47%	0.76%	0.16%	3.68%	5.17%	9.15%	10.79%	87.68%	19.11%	68.57%
2000	8.04%	5.42%	-8.52%	-6.03%	1.30%	2.42%	5.60%	1.51%	3.35%	2.78%	0.13%	2.53%	18.74%	-10.68%	29.42%
2001	5.24%	1.96%	3.52%	0.55%	3.14%	2.98%	3.74%	3.38%	-5.73%	1.38%	1.97%	1.91%	26.37%	-12.87%	39.24%
2002	3.33%	-3.35%	5.38%	2.70%	1.20%	9.17%	1.44%	1.51%	0.78%	0.14%	0.46%	1.33%	26.32%	-22.81%	49.13%
2003	4.57%	1.64%	-3.28%	3.16%	4.29%	4.08%	4.68%	5.21%	0.38%	5.56%	9.41%	5.51%	53.57%	26.12%	27.45%
2004	3.85%	7.49%	0.57%	-4.53%	3.56%	0.64%	-0.73%	-0.37%	0.19%	5.09%	3.31%	1.53%	22.02%	8.94%	13.08%
2005	4.91%	2.20%	2.47%	2.24%	1.16%	0.50%	-2.35%	-1.53%	1.30%	7.01%	1.86%	5.57%	27.99%	3.01%	24.98%
2006	0.90%	0.38%	2.36%	4.52%	3.58%	2.03%	2.09%	0.42%	0.51%	2.63%	-0.29%	0.45%	21.30%	13.74%	7.56%
2007	4.19%	0.35%	3.02%	1.60%	2.10%	-0.09%	3.49%	6.49%	0.68%	2.25%	-1.18%	0.60%	25.91%	3.24%	22.67%
2008	-0.56%	-0.06%	1.19%	1.70%	2.36%	-0.22%	8.18%	0.58%	3.35%	-5.65%	0.03%	0.03%	10.89%	-38.28%	49.17%
2009	1.03%	0.01%	0.31%	2.09%	5.43%	2.63%	-0.13%	4.75%	4.03%	-0.75%	0.81%	4.29%	27.14%	23.49%	3.65%
2010	-1.78%	7.16%	2.02%	1.01%	-0.17%	0.84%	0.77%	2.57%	1.68%	0.55%	-0.15%	2.27%	17.80%	12.84%	4.96%
2011	0.87%	-0.02%	-1.39%	0.31%	1.01%	-0.38%	0.63%	-6.61%	-0.33%	0.45%	0.02%	2.47%	-3.20%	-0.20%	-3.00%
2012	-0.62%	2.95%	-0.45%	-2.92%	0.46%	2.31%	0.69%	0.57%	2.22%	0.59%	2.29%	1.75%	10.12%	13.47%	-3.35%
2013	2.28%	2.49%	-1.14%	2.91%	0.97%	1.73%	2.24%	1.10%	3.32%	-2.76%	1.25%	0.91%	16.21%	29.69%	-13.48%
2014	0.12%	1.69%	-1.82%	0.05%	0.91%	2.78%	-0.75%	1.04%	-0.49%	-3.59%	-0.07%	0.94%	0.65%	11.29%	-10.64%
2015	-0.53%	1.45%	2.78%	-0.18%	2.87%	-1.11%	-0.01%	-0.72%	-0.55%	1.05%	0.30%	1.75%	7.22%	-0.81%	8.03%
2016	-1.60%	-0.72%	8.61%	0.15%	3.38%	-2.24%	2.58%	-1.69%	4.88%	0.47%	5.08%		19.92%	8.26%	11.67%

Example 1

Entry: Long at 26.64

Initial Stop Loss: 23.91

Exit: Two days later on open (slippage included)

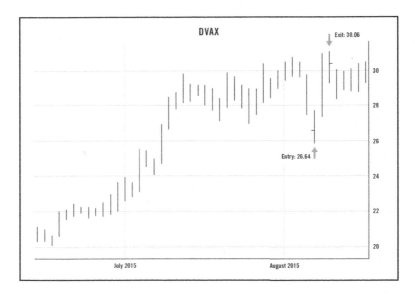

We see a clear uptrend lasting for a while, then before we enter, you could see a lot of fear. We like fear—we buy when there is a short-term pullback that implies there is a lot of fear. We put in a wide stop loss, which in this case wasn't reached, and we closed out the next day, with a solid gain. We hit our profit target and got out.

Example 2

Entry: Long at 3.21

Stop Loss: 2.29 (not shown)

Exit: Two days later at open, slippage included at 3.57

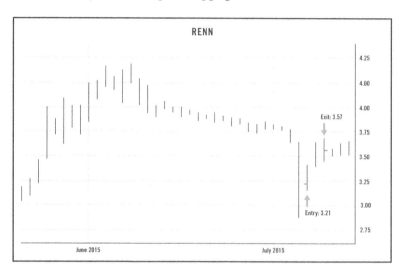

Again, we see a stock that was on a huge uptrend, when panic intervened, showing a pullback. That's our time to pounce. Our automated strategy tells us to buy while everyone is panicking. It's not easy for most people to buy at these points—there's probably a big, negative event in the news. People can't help but sell off at the sight of bad news, and that helps us. We love that fear—the more fear, the better.

Example 3 (Losing Trade)

Entry: Long at 7.25

Stop Loss: 6.60

Exit: Time exit after four days, market on close 6.94

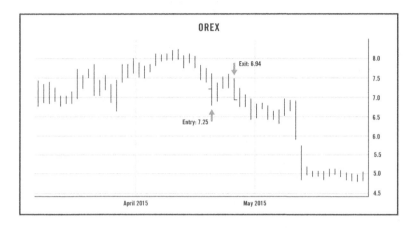

We entered on the same path here—uptrend, pullback due to fear, and then we pounce. The difference here was the stock never reached its profit target, nor was it stopped out. After four days, we accepted our loss (with a time stop) and sold. If we had stayed in, we would have lost more. This is why we always put in a time stop. A time stop tells us that this is not a good stock to be in, so we can then look for a better opportunity.

Example 4

Entry: Long at 29.82

Initial Stop Loss: 27.74

Exit: After profit target has been reached, third day market on open

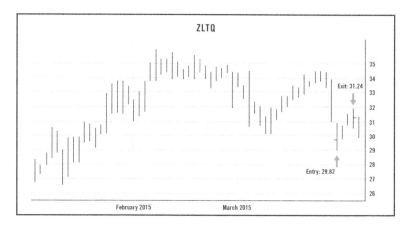

Here we see the same story again. Uptrend, panic, buy, large stop loss, and the stock shot up soon after. We got out the next day, market on open.

Summary

As you can see in the previous examples, the strategy is simple.

1. Look for an uptrend.
2. Look for significant volatility.
3. When the stock shows fear through a pullback, we buy even lower the next day.
4. We get out on a small target profit—we have a stop loss and a time stop.

The key to trading this strategy profitably is to have a large number of trades. The average profit per trade is not very high, so we need a large trade frequency to ensure large overall profits.

CHAPTER 10

Mean-Reversion Short— Make Money in Bad Markets

Most people don't want to be involved in short trading, because they're unfamiliar with it. However, it's a great way to capture profit in the markets. For people who are comfortable trading against the herd, won't have trouble ignoring the news, but want a different strategy than mean-reversion long, this is a great strategy.

This strategy is designed to make money when the market goes down. That's its biggest advantage, especially when used in concert with the mean-reversion long, or Weekly Rotation strategies. That's the ideal way to trade this strategy. They all work in perfect harmony, as I'll discuss in part 5.

Short strategies are a little less reliable than long strategies because shares to short are less available, and occasionally the government will ban selling stocks short. That has happened in big market panics—the government will say, "You can't short stocks right now." We have to be aware that could happen.

Also, there is no guarantee your broker will have the shares you need available to short.

More than 96 percent of my short trades in the past five years have been executed, so this isn't a huge issue, but you should be aware of it.

Objectives

- Trade short only on a large universe of stocks, taking advantage of overbought conditions by short selling the best stocks, and buying each back when it reverts to its mean.
- Execute in less than thirty minutes a day.
- Take advantage of stocks that have significant volatility and are on the shorter term overbought. By short selling these stocks, we get a strategy that performs well in bear markets and sideways markets.
- Beat the benchmarks, especially in bear markets.

Beliefs

This strategy is similar to the long mean-reversion strategy, but now we're looking for over*bought* situations, rather than over*sold* situations. Before we were buying short-term fear—now we're selling short-term greed.

When markets have shown irrational, fear-and-greed-based behavior, there is a statistically larger than normal probability that we will see a reaction in the opposite direction.

Markets are driven by fear and greed. To take advantage of this on the short side, we need to find greed-based situations. These stocks have been high-flying stocks, mostly in favor with

amateurs that have jumped on the fast-riding train. This typically is accompanied by large volatility.

In these situations, there will come a time when professional
traders will start to take profits. Statistically, there is an edge in
selling greed and buying it back when it has reverted or shown
some downward movement.

This kind of trading goes against human nature and is trading
against the herd. It is not easy to be a seller when everybody is
buying and when all news messages show panic, but it is exactly
what makes it a profitable strategy.

Since we are looking for shorter-term trades (a couple of
days), we need a large trade frequency. This is both done by
scanning over a large stock universe and creating exit rules in
which we get out fast.

Trading Universe (Same as Mean-Reversion Long)

- We trade all US stocks from AMEX, NASDAQ, and NYSE.
- We do not trade ETFs, pink sheets, or bulletin board stocks.
- For testing, this means that we take into account all listed
  and delisted stocks. Since 1995, this list consists of forty
  thousand stocks.

Filters

- Minimum Average Volume of the last twenty days is above
  500,000 shares.
- Minimum price is 10 USD.

Position Sizing
- Fixed fractional risk: 2 percent
- Maximum size: 10 percent

Entry Rules

It's essentially a mirror of the long strategy. The main difference is that we do *not* use an SMA filter. That's because we want to make sure this strategy assists our long strategies—this ensures that they work in harmony. Often the long strategy starts to lose money when the market is in an uptrend that starts to trend down, and this protects against both strategies losing money.

1. 7-day ADX: above 50
2. ATR% of past ten days: above 5 percent
3. The last two days were up days
4. 3-day RSI: above 85
   - This, combined with rule 3, is a measure of greed in the stock. That's what we're looking for. As the character Gordon Gecko said in the movie *Wall Street*, "Greed is good." There will come a moment when people sell, and that's when we'll profit.
5. When rules 1–4 apply, we place a maximum of ten orders.
6. We rank the orders by the highest three-day RSI.
   - The most overbought stocks indicate the most greed.
7. The following day, before the market opens, we place a limit order to sell short at an equal of the today's close.
8. At the end of the day, we look at which orders were filled.

9. If we want to use a stop loss on the first day, we need to watch the market the whole day and place the stop as explained in the previous example. Since we only want to work thirty minutes a day, we don't place stops on the days on which we trade the stock.

   ◻ Test results are similar, whether or not a stop loss is used on the first day.

Exit Rules

1. When an order gets filled, we place a stop loss after the close. The stop loss is 2.5 times the ten-day ATR, above the entry price. It is so wide because we sell fast-rising stocks, and mean reversion trades need space to develop.

2. We stay in the trade until any of the following conditions is met:

   a. Stop Loss: The trade gets stopped out.

   b. Profit Target: When the position has a profit of 4 percent or more, we exit next day, market on open.

   c. Time Exit: When two days have passed without A or B occurring, we exit market on close.

Ending Balance	3,602,653.94
CAGR%	17.79%
Max Total Equity DD	15.3%
Longest Drawdown	14.3
Wins	62.6%
Win/Loss Ratio	0.8
Average Days in Trade	1.70
R Squared	0.94
R Cubed	1.72
Ulcer Index	2.78

JAN 2, 1995 – NOV 23, 2016	TRADING SYSTEM	BENCHMARK
CAGR	17.79%	7.48%
Maximum Drawdown	15.33%	56.47%
Worst One Month Return	-7.34%	-16.52%
Worst One Day Return	-6.25%	-9.84%
Annualized Volatility	11.50%	19.31%
Average Exposure	13.66%	100.00%
Sharpe	1.55	0.39
MAR	1.16	0.13
Daily Return Correlation to Benchmark	-0.24	1.00
YTD Return	15.69%	8.26%
MTD Return	4.75%	3.83%
Total Return	3502.65%	385.05%

Here we see the same characteristics as the long strategy—a high win rate, low exposure, low trade duration, and also a low ulcer index. The results are superb.

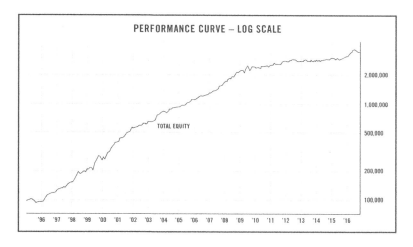

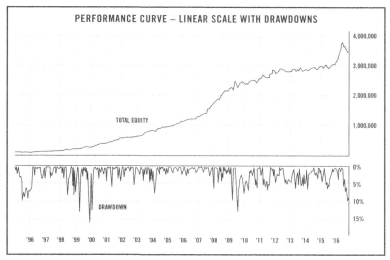

Again, if you compare with the long strategy, they are perfect complements. The short strategy is great in bear markets (2000–2002, 2008), as you can see. In times of poor performance (2012–2013), the long strategy did great.

	JAN	FEB	MAR	APR	MAY	JUN	JUL	AUG	SEP	OCT	NOV	DEC	ANNUAL	SPY	COMPARISON
1995	0.32%	2.19%	-1.06%	0.96%	-1.19%	-1.37%	-5.14%	0.27%	2.19%	0.10%	-1.81%	0.10%	-4.56%	35.16%	-39.73%
1996	1.93%	2.75%	3.38%	9.14%	1.92%	1.10%	1.35%	1.60%	1.28%	-2.01%	1.93%	0.96%	28.06%	20.31%	7.74%
1997	4.91%	0.89%	1.91%	-1.05%	3.53%	-0.05%	2.75%	3.43%	0.85%	4.93%	0.66%	-0.39%	24.55%	31.39%	-6.84%
1998	3.92%	3.16%	5.33%	9.98%	2.95%	-5.50%	2.45%	1.52%	2.84%	-2.44%	9.12%	-4.75%	31.05%	27.04%	4.01%
1999	4.84%	2.48%	2.09%	-4.29%	10.80%	2.58%	8.43%	5.81%	5.76%	-3.98%	1.39%	-6.90%	31.23%	19.11%	12.12%
2000	3.82%	0.89%	6.42%	4.84%	2.27%	6.45%	6.87%	-0.07%	5.21%	4.98%	0.43%	-0.99%	49.22%	-10.68%	59.90%
2001	2.47%	7.70%	2.39%	-1.69%	4.91%	4.73%	3.77%	0.64%	1.80%	5.70%	3.17%	-0.56%	40.72%	-12.87%	53.59%
2002	2.48%	1.76%	0.46%	0.41%	0.88%	0.48%	0.39%	4.68%	0.14%	0.03%	0.69%	3.07%	16.50%	-22.81%	39.30%
2003	0.01%	-0.80%	0.46%	1.42%	-0.43%	10.47%	8.21%	-0.97%	2.83%	6.07%	-0.41%	1.58%	31.46%	26.12%	5.34%
2004	-0.61%	-4.11%	0.66%	7.47%	0.03%	-0.26%	3.30%	1.60%	1.44%	1.33%	-0.61%	-0.84%	9.38%	8.94%	0.44%
2005	0.41%	3.13%	2.29%	-0.29%	0.07%	3.32%	0.14%	1.98%	2.04%	5.43%	0.84%	-0.56%	20.30%	3.01%	17.28%
2006	1.16%	1.73%	0.29%	4.31%	0.75%	0.29%	0.69%	0.15%	0.55%	-0.59%	3.48%	1.89%	15.60%	13.74%	1.86%
2007	1.43%	2.38%	1.07%	2.00%	-0.03%	1.21%	3.42%	6.90%	0.82%	1.21%	3.78%	3.87%	31.72%	3.24%	28.48%
2008	1.32%	4.71%	1.79%	0.05%	5.57%	1.21%	0.12%	3.74%	5.37%	-1.25%	0.83%	2.76%	29.27%	-38.28%	67.55%
2009	1.62%	1.48%	-4.48%	3.87%	7.93%	3.01%	-7.34%	0.53%	4.67%	0.97%	-2.12%	-1.60%	7.87%	23.49%	-15.62%
2010	1.42%	0.86%	-1.78%	2.58%	1.22%	0.71%	-0.40%	0.85%	-1.25%	-0.73%	1.33%	1.88%	6.80%	12.84%	-6.05%
2011	2.05%	1.18%	1.66%	-1.05%	-2.06%	1.29%	1.16%	-0.08%	5.46%	2.15%	2.32%	-0.21%	11.92%	-0.20%	12.12%
2012	-3.24%	2.24%	-0.32%	2.87%	-0.22%	0.74%	0.10%	-2.93%	0.25%	-1.18%	0.54%	0.02%	-1.49%	13.47%	14.97%
2013	-0.44%	1.99%	1.91%	-1.37%	-1.12%	1.03%	-2.92%	4.84%	-3.16%	1.82%	0.58%	-2.38%	0.48%	26.69%	29.21%
2014	2.97%	-2.67%	2.42%	0.06%	0.84%	-0.11%	1.39%	-0.19%	-1.18%	0.26%	1.20%	1.88%	6.94%	11.29%	-4.35%
2015	0.07%	1.90%	3.15%	-2.96%	-1.27%	0.07%	-0.37%	1.99%	1.04%	0.35%	1.88%	2.69%	4.95%	-0.81%	5.46%
2016	0.98%	3.54%	4.68%	2.95%	4.55%	0.47%	-2.01%	-2.45%	-2.58%	0.22%	4.75%		15.69%	8.26%	7.43%

Example 1

Entry: Sell short at 15.00.

Initial Stop Loss: 17.27

Exit: 14.31

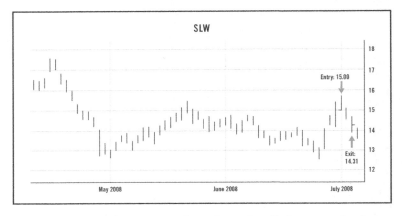

The story is simple. We see a lot of greed, sell short, with a large stop loss, and capture a quick profit. This was a significant win.

Example 2

Entry: Sell short at 63.50.

Initial Stop Loss: 81.12 (not shown)

Exit: The following day, at 57.91

In about a week, the stock moved from 45 USD to 65 USD, which signaled greed. Again, we saw that greed, and we captured gains. There was a fast reaction downward, as expected.

Example 3 (Loss)

Entry: Sell short at 35.02.

Initial Stop Loss: 40.05

Close: 37.37

This was closed with a loss, but as you can see, we did not come near getting stopped out. The time stop closed out this position.

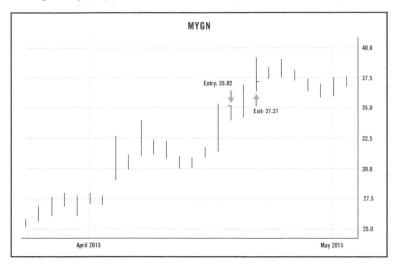

We sold a lot of greed again, but it turned out greed hadn't yet hit its peak. Our time stop saved us.

Example 4

Entry: Sell short at 12.22.

Stop Loss: 14.84 (not shown)

Exit: Close at 10.79.

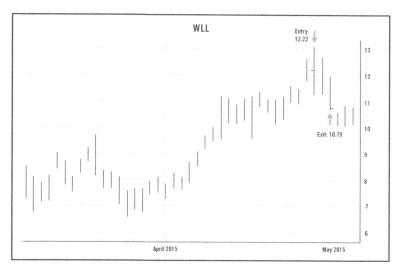

Here's one more example of selling greed, and its paying off.

PART 5

The Exponential Magic of Combining Strategies

Weekly Rotation + Mean-Reversion Short—Trend Following without Big Drawdowns

If you like trend following, but can't handle the large drawdowns paired with it, this is a good strategy for you.

The idea is to combine lots of open, long positions with short-term mean reversion strategies. By doing that, our drawdowns are lower. Trend following alone saw a 30 percent drawdown; now we're at 23 percent. In addition, CAGR increased from 19 percent to 26 percent.

We're combining two directions (long and short) with two styles (trend following and mean reversion).

Here's a chart comparing them when used alone, versus in concert.

STRATEGY:	CAGR	MAX DD	TOTAL RETURN	LARGEST DD IN MONTHS	SHARPE RATIO	VOLATILITY
Weekly Rotation long	19.71%	30%	4908%	38	0.96	20.54%
Mean-Reversion Short	17.79%	15%	3502%	14	1.55	11.47%
Weekly Rotation + Mean-Reversion Short	26.32%	23%	16,545%	16	1.41	18.61%

As you can see, they work incredibly well together. By adding the mean-reversion short strategy to the Weekly Rotation, the CAGR increased almost 7 percent, while the maximum drawdown decreased 7 percent, and its duration was cut from thirty-eight months to sixteen. That's a tremendous improvement.

Ending Balance	**16,644,425.74**
CAGR%	26.32%
Max Total Equity DD	23.6%
Longest Drawdown	15.6%
Wins	60.6%
Win/Loss Ratio	1.1
Winning Months	68.82%
R Squared	0.96
R Cubed	1.32
Ulcer Index	6.10

JAN 2, 1995 – NOV 23, 2016	TRADING SYSTEM	BENCHMARK
CAGR	26.32%	7.48%
Maximum Drawdown	23.62%	56.47%
Worst One Month Return	-11.38%	-16.52%
Worst One Day Return	-7.68%	-9.84%
Annualized Volatility	18.60%	19.31%
Sharpe	1.41	0.39
MAR	1.11	0.13
Daily Return Correlation to Benchmark	0.41	1.00
YTD Return	13.39%	8.26%
MTD Return	8.58%	3.83%
Total Return	**16,545.60%**	**385.05%**

The strategy beats the benchmark quite easily. Drawdowns are shorter than with the uncombined strategies, and their magnitude is lower. The win rate is lower than the combined long and short mean reversion strategy, but that's expected—because trend following strategies have a lower win rate, but larger win-loss ratio.

Most importantly, this strategy beats the benchmark by a large magnitude, with low correlation.

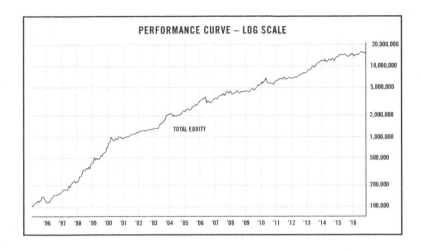

PERFORMANCE CURVE – LOG SCALE

TOTAL EQUITY

Again, when one strategy is down, the other is up, and vice versa. In the bear markets of 2000–2003, when the trend-following strategy was flat, this strategy continued to make money.

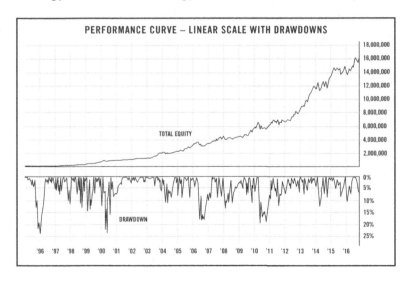

PERFORMANCE CURVE – LINEAR SCALE WITH DRAWDOWNS

TOTAL EQUITY

DRAWDOWN

There are some sharp drawdowns—that's what happens when the long-term trend following strategy was making a lot of money beforehand. We have to give money back, because we've profited handsomely. That's a consequence of trend following. However, by combining strategies, these drawdowns are much smaller than they were with trend following only.

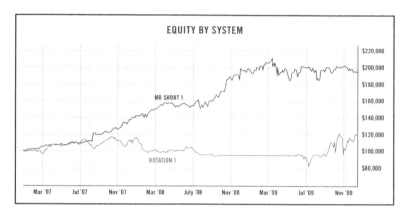

When one is flat, the other makes money. In 2008, the Weekly Rotation was losing, then flat—but the short strategy was making great money. Since 2012, the short strategy hasn't done much, but the Weekly Rotation has skyrocketed. In the beginning of 2015, the Weekly Rotation started to give back profits—and the short strategy started to make profits again. They balance each other out perfectly.

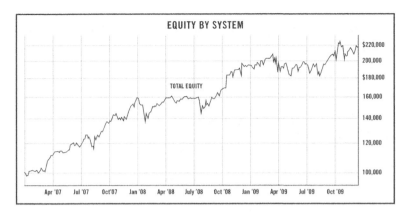

In 1999, the strategy made over 100 percent! As expected, it gave money back afterward (the consequence of trend following), but not nearly as much as if we had been only long invested. It wound up making a profit in 2000—this is a great combination.

In 2008, that horrid year for the index, the strategy was a slight minus, but destroyed the benchmark.

By combining long-term trend following and short-term mean reversion, we make money in bull markets, bear markets, *and* sideways markets. We make money in all markets.

This strategy is great when you want to make big gains in bull years, but you still want protection for when the market goes down. It's a phenomenal combo.

	JAN	FEB	MAR	APR	MAY	JUN	JUL	AUG	SEP	OCT	NOV	DEC	ANNUAL	SPY	COMPARISON
1995	1.95%	7.43%	0.84%	2.35%	0.75%	5.36%	2.23%	5.63%	3.29%	-3.80%	-9.51%	-5.75%	9.82%	35.16%	-25.34%
1996	4.01%	4.95%	2.49%	10.60%	3.93%	1.17%	-0.40%	4.32%	0.39%	-0.36%	4.67%	0.47%	42.18%	20.31%	21.87%
1997	13.51%	-4.73%	-1.32%	3.44%	7.56%	-0.45%	14.10%	1.86%	4.95%	-4.47%	2.10%	-1.52%	38.50%	31.39%	7.11%
1998	9.46%	12.28%	2.18%	15.45%	2.45%	2.16%	5.05%	-5.59%	15.47%	-1.44%	3.30%	6.55%	88.51%	27.04%	61.46%
1999	23.63%	-9.73%	8.62%	-6.04%	2.61	7.64%	5.28%	7.49%	0.35%	4.69%	11.52%	20.65%	101.20%	19.11%	82.10%
2000	-5.52%	25.89%	-1.73%	-2.56%	-11.31%	10.15%	-1.59%	14.13%	-3.82%	-3.52%	-0.48%	0.32%	15.75%	-10.68%	26.43%
2001	-0.12%	2.82%	1.37%	-0.82%	2.60%	2.92%	2.05%	0.47%	0.99%	3.18%	1.62%	0.90%	20.60%	-12.87%	33.48%
2002	3.95%	1.19%	1.03%	0.29%	-0.75	0.35%	0.14%	2.75%	0.14%	0.37%	0.37%	1.85%	12.23%	-22.81%	35.04%
2003	0.05%	-0.53%	0.07%	7.26%	5.69%	3.34%	4.49%	7.99%	4.42%	14.41%	3.14%	-0.79%	60.93%	26.12%	34.81%
2004	3.21%	-1.86%	-3.93%	-3.40%	3.38%	1.13%	2.08%	-1.36%	2.72%	3.22%	8.58%	1.38%	15.49%	8.94%	6.55%
2005	-0.68%	5.90%	-1.25%	-5.22%	6.15%	3.27%	4.48%	5.62%	4.53%	-1.33	2.46%	1.17%	27.33%	3.01%	24.32%
2006	12.31%	-1.13%	6.49%	-0.39%	-5.82%	1.94%	-6.87%	-4.03%	-0.37%	6.64%	3.96%	1.29%	13.09%	13.74%	-0.65%
2007	1.31%	-2.79%	8.41%	2.47%	3.62%	-0.85%	3.85%	1.15%	6.29%	0.95%	-1.89%	6.40%	32.26%	3.24%	29.02%
2008	-11.38%	3.29%	-0.03%	0.32%	4.73%	2.21%	-6.55%	2.67%	2.29%	-0.68%	0.49%	1.75%	-2.06%	-38.28%	36.22%
2009	0.85%	1.04%	-3.10%	2.54%	5.00%	0.68%	-1.75%	2.46%	8.59%	-4.46%	4.81%	6.25%	24.48%	23.49%	0.99%
2010	4.94%	5.63%	4.26%	-0.69%	-6.32%	-5.40%	0.35%	0.90%	-0.36%	-1.35%	4.92%	3.03%	9.43%	12.84%	-3.41%
2011	3.39%	3.86%	5.97%	-0.17%	-0.33%	-1.37%	3.08%	-6.50%	0.22%	3.92%	2.60%	-3.44%	11.04%	-0.20%	11.24%
2012	-2.30%	4.36%	1.77%	-0.69%	1.61%	7.43%	-0.09%	1.34%	4.25%	1.67%	0.11%	1.23%	22.32%	13.47%	8.84%
2013	7.39%	-0.77%	5.96%	0.68%	5.83%	-2.14%	8.41%	0.79%	4.39%	4.09%	4.12%	-1.26%	43.70%	29.69%	14.01%
2014	-0.04%	4.84%	-5.49%	-2.03%	4.63%	4.81%	-4.19%	4.14%	0.52%	-1.84%	6.46%	1.25%	12.92%	11.29%	1.63%
2015	3.38%	5.63%	1.19%	-4.30%	5.03%	-1.93%	-0.74%	-3.35%	-0.42%	2.70%	3.38%	-0.66%	9.74%	-0.81%	10.55%
2016	-4.92%	0.71%	2.82%	-1.44%	3.30%	2.68%	5.48%	-0.57%	1.15%	-4.36%	8.58%		13.39%	8.26%	5.13%

Mean-Reversion Long and Short Combined— Lower Risk, Higher Upside

This strategy combines both the mean-reversion long strategy and the mean-reversion short. We trade them simultaneously. The result, as you'll see, is that the CAGR increases significantly, and the max drawdown is significantly lower. That means you lower the risk, while gaining upside!

When one strategy starts to lose money, the other makes up for it. The long position starts to lose money, but the short positions recover those losses. It balances things out, and performance is exponentially better than using either one alone. We trade both strategies at 100 percent equity, when possible. I don't mind trading 100 percent both when I can, because by being 100 percent long and 100 percent short, I'm basically market neutral. Sometimes we will be more directionally invested—say, 70 percent long or 70 percent short instead—and that's fine, too.

When you trade mean-reversion long by itself, there will be times when it's completely flat. That means you're not making great use of your capital. By trading both simultaneously, you better use your capital and take advantage of the fact that the two strategies are designed for two different market types, so you're covered in all scenarios.

Here's a table comparing the two strategies being used alone, versus together.

MEAN REVERSION LONG AND SHORT COMBINED

Ending Balance	18,692,897.21
CAGR%	26.99%
Max Total Equity DD	11.5%
Longest Drawdown	15.9
Wins	65.2%
Win/Loss Ratio	0.8
Average Days in Trade	2.00
Long Profit Contribution	67.74%
Short Profit Contribution	32.26%
Winning Months	80.61%
R Squared	0.95
R Cubed	4.07
Ulcer Index	2.04

JAN 2, 1995 – NOV 23, 2016	TRADING SYSTEM	BENCHMARK
CAGR	26.99%	7.48%
Maximum Drawdown	11.46%	56.47%
Worst One Month Return	-6.31%	-16.52%
Worst One Day Return	-5.79%	-9.84%
Annualized Volatility	1-.51%	19.31%
Sharpe	2.57	0.39
MAR	2.36	0.13
Daily Return Correlation to Benchmark	0.12	1.00
YTD Return	22.09%	8.26%
MTD Return	5.67%	3.83%
Total Return	**18,592.90%**	**385.05%**

As you can see, the MAR ratio (CAGR divided by biggest drawdown) is excellent—and there's almost no correlation with the benchmark.

Because it's a mean reversion strategy, the average days in a trade is low, and you need a lot of trades. This strategy outperforms the benchmark exponentially—about four times more, with five times lower drawdowns! That's the magic of combining noncorrelated strategy, getting maximum bang for your buck. There is a low Ulcer index, high R-cubed, and over 80 percent of months are profitable.

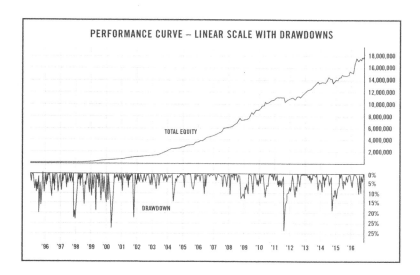

As you can see, the drawdowns don't last long. We recover quickly, because trade frequency is high, and therefore opportunities abound. The pace helps you.

The largest drawdown of the long strategy was about 20 percent, but by combining strategies, it shrunk to 11 percent. The CAGR of the long strategy was 21 percent—by combining strategies, it increased to 26 percent.

The strategy has been profitable every year since 1995, even in the big bear market of 2008, when it performed 64 percent better than the S&P 500. There are only a few years in which the index outperformed this powerful strategy.

Recently, results have been mild, but that's because volatility has been low. That leads some people to conclude that mean reversion no longer works, but that's ridiculous. We *know* that low volatility equals mild results with mean reversion. You can see that in our trading rules. We simply don't get enough trade setups, which means we don't have lots of opportunities to create short-term profits.

Risk-adjusted returns are still good, but our net results are underwhelming. We don't have enough volatility to see a large-enough volume of trades. Once volatility starts to structurally increase, our mean reversion strategies will see better results.

In the following table, you can see the results of all described strategies—including the benchmark (buy and hold of the S&P 500).

STRATEGY:	CAGR%	MAX DD	TOTAL RETURN	LARGEST DD IN MONTHS	SHARPE RATIO
SPY Buy & Hold	7.48%	56%	385%	86	0.39
Weekly Rotation long	19.71%	30%	4,908%	38	0.96
Mean-reversion long	21.92%	20%	7,557%	14	2.15
Mean-reversion short	17.79%	15%	3,502%	14	1.54
Mean-reversion long/short combined	26.99%	11%	18,592%	16	2.54
Weekly Rotation + mean-reversion short	26.32%	23%	16,545%	16	1.43

Clearly, all of the quantified strategies have a clear and consistent edge, and combining them increases that edge exponentially.

	JAN	FEB	MAR	APR	MAY	JUN	JUL	AUG	SEP	OCT	NOV	DEC	ANNUAL	SPY	COMPARISON
1995	0.97%	2.50%	-1.79%	-0.36%	-0.34%	0.47%	-3.64%	-0.72%	4.67%	6.70%	-1.00%	0.64%	7.94%	35.16%	-27.22%
1996	1.86%	4.01%	2.72%	8.20%	1.10%	10.28%	1.73%	2.74%	2.17%	0.21%	1.94%	1.83%	45.81%	20.31%	25.50%
1997	4.83%	2.01%	2.68%	-0.55%	4.56%	-0.96%	3.31%	4.63%	3.72%	-1.64%	1.02%	1.46%	27.81%	31.39%	-3.58%
1998	5.29%	3.72%	6.02%	11.95%	3.32%	-4.07%	2.52%	1.68%	3.82%	-0.85%	7.80%	2.55%	52.38%	27.04%	25.33%
1999	10.93%	3.09%	8.59%	2.33%	9.31%	3.78%	4.79%	2.62%	6.30%	2.10%	6.68%	-0.99%	77.71%	19.11%	58.60%
2000	8.44%	5.32%	-4.15%	-2.07%	2.42%	5.36%	8.77%	1.13%	6.15%	3.62%	-0.30%	0.81%	40.68%	-10.68%	51.36%
2001	5.87%	5.52%	3.98%	-0.71%	5.16%	4.40%	5.15%	2.93%	-3.48%	4.20%	2.96%	0.29%	42.32%	-12.87%	55.20%
2002	3.97%	-0.87%	4.90%	2.10%	1.12%	8.19%	0.48%	3.83%	0.55%	0.35%	0.68%	2.64%	31.35%	-22.81%	54.16%
2003	3.26%	0.75%	-2.08%	2.25%	2.77%	8.10%	7.44%	3.57%	1.79%	7.03%	6.89%	5.04%	57.52%	26.12%	31.40%
2004	2.72%	4.64%	1.14%	-1.01%	3.19%	0.42%	1.01%	0.33%	0.54%	4.95%	2.72%	0.56%	23.17%	8.94%	14.23%
2005	5.21%	3.01%	3.09%	2.00%	0.94%	1.83%	-2.00%	-0.01%	1.95%	8.60%	1.73%	4.43%	35.01%	3.01%	32.00%
2006	1.15%	0.25%	2.18%	5.59%	4.00%	1.83%	2.25%	0.33%	0.63%	2.20%	0.64%	0.96%	24.21%	13.74%	10.47%
2007	4.32%	0.98%	2.87%	1.96%	1.80%	0.43%	3.49%	7.51%	0.85%	2.27%	0.01%	1.80%	31.97%	3.24%	28.73%
2008	-0.89%	1.53%	1.65%	1.40%	4.28%	0.39%	7.54%	1.97%	4.78%	-5.04%	0.31%	1.06%	20.08%	-38.28%	58.36%
2009	1.03%	0.63%	-1.65%	4.07%	7.16%	2.82%	-3.40%	4.77%	5.14%	-0.72%	-0.36%	3.12%	24.45%	23.49%	0.96%
2010	-1.03%	0.94%	1.05%	2.06%	0.09%	0.82%	0.72%	2.83%	0.99%	0.20%	0.37%	2.84%	18.68%	12.84%	5.84%
2011	1.38%	0.94%	-0.68%	-0.08%	0.22%	-0.05%	0.14%	-6.31%	1.67%	1.08%	0.80%	1.45%	0.30%	-0.20%	0.50%
2012	-1.46%	3.65%	-0.55%	-2.07%	0.42%	2.00%	0.41%	-0.48%	2.04%	0.10%	2.21%	1.76%	8.15%	13.47%	-5.32%
2013	1.65%	3.09%	-0.37%	2.04%	0.21%	1.98%	1.13%	2.48%	2.15%	-2.06%	1.07%	0.02%	14.12%	29.69%	-15.57%
2014	0.56%	0.50%	-0.97%	1.28%	1.09%	2.34%	-0.16%	0.78%	-0.42%	-3.06%	0.37%	1.49%	3.76%	11.29%	-7.53%
2015	-0.47%	0.66%	3.69%	-1.06%	2.76%	-0.81%	-0.26%	0.26%	-0.19%	1.06%	0.70%	2.68%	9.25%	-0.81%	10.07%
2016	-1.26%	0.14%	9.10%	0.91%	5.18%	-1.86%	1.45%	-2.68%	3.61%	0.51%	5.67%		22.09%	8.26%	13.84%

I personally trade a suite of twelve noncorrelated strategies, and I train most of my clients to combine all of the described strategies, if it suits their personality. The more proven strategies you combine, the higher your risk-adjusted performance. Combining all proven strategies is fairly easy to scale, and then you can have the option of adding more, later. When it comes to automated training, it truly is "the more, the merrier." Each added strategy increases upside while decreasing risk.

PART 6

Conclusion—The Final Steps to Financial Freedom

The Missing Ingredient—Position-Sizing (To Achieve Your Objectives)

As mentioned before, through position sizing, you define your objectives. First, your strategy needs an edge. Once you have an edge, position size is the missing ingredient, enabling you to trade your strategy according to your objectives and within your comfort zone.

There are many ways to define your position sizing, based on your objectives, risk tolerance, and whether or not you'll trade on margin.

The variety of models is beyond the scope of this book, so I'll show some simple adjustments, based on profit objectives and risk tolerance. Through the following example, you can see how position sizing affects both CAGR and maximum drawdown. For the purpose of this example, we'll use the combined suite of long and short mean reversion. Remember: We're trading 100 percent long and 100 percent short.

The results of trading long and short mean reversion

combined are these:

- *CAGR:* 26 percent
- *Max Drawdown:* 11 percent
- *Risk per Trade:* 2 percent
- *Maximum Positions:* Ten long and Ten short
- *Maximum Size per Position:* 10 percent of total equity

The Conservative-Sizing Model

Now, here's an example of a strategy for the more conservative trader. This strategy is for someone who likes combining long and short mean reversion, but can't stomach the daily and monthly swings and drawdowns. They're too large, and he or she won't be able to follow his or her strategy. The following is a simple adaptation for traders with a lower risk tolerance.

We basically cut our sizing in half:

- We trade the same amount of positions—a maximum of ten long positions and ten short.
- Risk per Trade: 1 percent
- Maximum Size per Position: 5 percent
- Since this is long and short combined, we can get up to 50 percent long exposure and 50 percent short (10 positions x 5% of equity).

RESULTS CONSERVATIVE POSITION SIZING

JAN 2, 1995 – NOV 23, 2016	TRADING SYSTEM	BENCHMARK
CAGR	14.78%	7.48%
Maximum Drawdown	5.62%	56.47%
Worst One Month Return	-2.95%	-16.52%
Worst One Day Return	-2.93%	-9.84%
Annualized Volatility	5.46%	19.31%
Sharpe	2.71	0.39
MAR	2.63	0.13
Daily Return Correlation to Benchmark	0.08	1.00
YTD Return	10.60%	8.26%
MTD Return	2.92%	3.83%
Total Return	**1,944.36%**	**385.05%**

See how the drawdowns lower from 11.6 percent to 5.6 percent? We take a hit on the CAGR, of course, but we've chosen that. The CAGR is still 14.6 percent—double the CAGR of the S&P 500, and the drawdown is almost ten times lower! The lower the risk, the lower the CAGR.

The Aggressive-Sizing Model

- ◻ Now let's take a very aggressive model, where we trade significantly on margin. This position sizing isn't possible to trade at some brokers, but at mine, Interactive Brokers, this option is available to portfolios above $125,000 USD, using portfolio margin.
- ◻ We trade the same amount of positions—a maximum of ten long positions and ten short.
- ◻ Risk per Trade: 3 percent
- ◻ Maximum Size per Position: 15 percent
- ◻ Since this is long and short combined, we can theoretically get up to 150 percent long exposure and 150 percent short (10 positions x 15% of equity).

RESULTS AGGRESSIVE POSITION SIZING

JAN 2, 1995 – NOV 23, 2016	TRADING SYSTEM	BENCHMARK
CAGR	39.61%	7.48%
Maximum Drawdown	16.52%	56.47%
Worst One Month Return	-9.83%	-16.52%
Worst One Day Return	-9.07%	-9.84%
Annualized Volatility	15.56%	19.31%
Sharpe	2.55	0.39
MAR	2.14	0.13
Daily Return Correlation to Benchmark	0.15	1.00
YTD Return	34.12%	8.26%
MTD Return	8.41%	3.83%
Total Return	148,670.46%	385.05%

The CAGR goes through the roof, at around 40 percent annually, but of course the drawdown increases as well. Still, at 18 percent, it is more than three times lower than that of the S&P 500. As always, seeking more profit requires you to risk more.

I do not recommend trading these position sizes—most people will overestimate their risk appetite. This example was provided as a guideline to see what the impact on your overall returns and drawdowns are when you use a different position-sizing algorithm.

Summary

There are many more advanced techniques to achieve your objectives through position sizing, but that's a little beyond the scope of this book. There are many options, and you'll find one that suits you.

Here is a comparison of different position sizing models:

STRATEGY:	CAGR	MAX DD	TOTAL RETURN
Standard sizing - Mean-reversion long/ short combined	26.99%	11%	18,592%
Conservative sizing	14.78%	5.62%	1,944%
Aggressive sizing:	39.61%	18.52%	148,670%

CHAPTER 14

Turn It Loose—But Watch Out for This Pitfall

Most people wonder, *These strategies look great—but are they exactly what I'll get in the future?* It's important to understand that back tests are representations of the past, based on past data. They are not guarantees of future results.

There is only one guarantee about the markets—they *always* change. We'll always have bull markets, bear markets, sideways markets, and different levels of volatility. If you have a strategy that takes all of this into account and is based on your beliefs, you will do well. That said, your results will vary based on market conditions.

I cannot promise perfect results, but I can promise that if you follow the steps outlined in the book, you'll beat 90 percent of traders.

There will come a time when your largest tested drawdown will be exceeded. The same will happen for your longest drawdown. That's the reality of trading. This sounds easy to handle, but if you have a tested drawdown of 15 percent, which took ten months to recover from, many people will see a drawdown of 17.5 percent for thirteen months and panic. They think their strategy is broken, because the "maximum drawdown" was exceeded. But the key word is *tested*. The past can approximate the future, but back tests are not perfect. Of course, the people panicking still have a good strategy. It's not broken. The problem is with their psychology. You mustn't have your judgment clouded by looking at your bank account. In the worst of times, still follow the strategy!

However, the converse will happen. There will be times when volatility is so high that your mean reversion strategies go nuts, and you make more money than expected. There will be another time like the dot-com bubble, and your Weekly Rotation strategy will go crazy. There will be good times, and there will be bad times. But you'll be better prepared than almost anybody.

You will succeed long term if you're consistent in following your strategy.

Remember the steps to trading profitably.

First, define your beliefs. Are you a trend follower? Are you using mean reversion? Are you combining them to increase their effectiveness? Define this, and be crystal clear. Then, make your objectives as clear as possible.

Next, define your position sizing and cut it in half to be safe—at least at the beginning of your trading.

Trading should be treated as a business. It's your money, so be serious about it. Have a plan.

Finally, execute consistently. You can have a great strategy, but if you don't trade it perfectly, you'll turn a winning strategy into a losing one. You must follow your rules and refrain from overriding strategies. Ignore the news. Overreacting makes your strategies useless.

I have seen many people who have great strategies with perfect trading rules and a clear edge, but their psychology is in conflict. They can't avoid looking at the news, and the outside noise clouds their thoughts and leads them to ignore the computer's orders on certain days. They don't trade when the strategy says they should. Most of the time, they missed out on trades that saw great returns. They turn a great strategy into a useless strategy because they don't have the discipline to trade it consistently. Consistency is key.

If you've followed the step-by-step approach—first defining your beliefs, second, your rules, third, automating your strategy, and fourth, trading it—you have succeeded in creating a consistent, scientifically proven way to make money investing for the rest of your life. You're on the path to create financial and emotional freedom—no more stress.

You can, in other words, finally relax.

The only way you can fail is if you haven't defined your beliefs, objectives, and position sizing thoroughly. I can't emphasize this enough—trading is virtually all psychology. You can have the perfect strategy, but if it doesn't suit your beliefs, you will override it, and it will be useless.

It's hard work to create the strategy, but once you've done it, the hard work is done. It's hard work to define your beliefs, strengths, objectives, and exact strategies, and do the testing. But when you're done, the process of executing your strategy is effortless. Everything is automated. It takes a half hour a day to achieve effortless financial freedom. You just need to follow the process every day, and check in occasionally to ensure your real-time results match your back testing—that nothing has changed.

Most people don't understand the importance of the initial hard work, though, or they aren't strong enough to be honest with themselves and admit their weaknesses.

If people are unclear in defining their trading style, objectives, and position sizing, they override their strategies. That leads to disaster. Their strategy has a clear edge—like the ones I've presented in this book, and executed myself—but they don't follow it. They don't trade every day. Or, often, they'll do a great job for the first three months, but when a drawdown hits, they'll start doubting their strategy, because they're emotionally attached to the money they're losing.

If that's the case, then they didn't define their objectives correctly. Drawdowns shouldn't affect you, because we have planned for drawdowns in the strategy's creation process. If you're going to doubt your strategy and ignore the proven signals, your strategy becomes useless. It's useless to put in so much work only to not follow the strategy and fail. You must be honest with yourself beforehand, then trust and follow the strategy to the letter.

I had one client who was an experienced, skilled trader, but used a fundamental approach. He contacted me because he wanted to shift to a technical and automated approach. We developed a great strategy that I could have used myself. That's how great it was! Yet I checked in with him six months later, and he said he "wasn't doing well"; he was down 10 percent. That was strange, because market conditions had been favorable for his particular strategy. I asked him to send me a back test, and it showed a *profit* of 10 percent. There was a 20 percent gap. I asked him what the problem was. He should have been happily making money.

He told me he had gotten "really uncomfortable" when he had his first drawdown, which had only been 10 percent. He skipped a couple of trades that he didn't like. Of course, they turned out the complete opposite. He missed all of those profits, and instead of a 10 percent profit, he was on a 10 percent loss after just six months. He didn't trust the strategy, because he hadn't been honest up front about his risk tolerance. His position sizing wasn't suiting his stomach. He couldn't handle it, and he started to doubt the strategy.

He has overcome it now, but only because I worked with him to completely redefine his objectives. We didn't change the strategy. The strategy was phenomenal. We needed to redefine his objectives, so that he could trade his strategy under all circumstances, in a clear and relaxed mental state. We designed a new position-sizing strategy that actually suited his risk profile, and now he can actually follow the strategy and execute all of the trades.

Now, it's working well, and he is making consistent, double-digit annual returns with low volatility. He follows his strategy consistently, and he's happy.

In my experience with managing other people's money, nine times out of ten, people cannot handle the drawdowns they say they can handle. I trade for some of my customers, and I have to be extra cautious to be sure I understand their true risk tolerance. For certain people, I'll only use low-volatility strategies because I want to ensure I'm within their risk-tolerance parameters. I don't want people feeling anxious about their money, calling me up, and freaking out about a temporary drawdown. My objectives don't matter. Perhaps a different strategy or more aggressive position sizing would have higher upside, but if it's going to make the client an emotional mess, it's too risky. What matters is the client's objectives and what he or she can truly handle.

Whenever a client first defines his desired position sizing, I tell him to cut it in half, then see how it goes. When you look at your strategy's back test, you see the equity curve rising from the lower left quadrant to the top right—you see yourself making money long term. It all looks so good and simple. But that equity curve doesn't show your feelings when it suddenly goes down, and real money is on the line. Your retirement savings have been shaved down. Whatever you think you can handle in your current, clear mental state, cut it in half. Start there, and you can adjust later.

This is a lifelong approach, so take it slow. If you think you can easily handle a drawdown of up to 20 percent, start with an algorithm that can only get to 10 percent. You'll be infinitely more comfortable. When you begin to observe your feelings while you're trading, and when you've done it for a consistent time period and *proven* you can handle certain drawdowns, then you can move up. This way of trading is intended to set you up for life. It's not about maximizing profits right away. The first six months aren't important or profitable. It's important to use those six months to develop the ability, skill, and comfort to follow your strategy and achieve financial freedom for life.

Your beliefs need to be based on real-life experience. If you say you can handle a drawdown of 20 percent, what real-life experience is it based on? Everybody's circumstances are different. Do you only have your life savings and no other income, or do you earn $25,000 a month on top of your $100,000 of trading capital? If you have that monthly income, you can be more lenient with your risk tolerance. You're still covered. If that's not the case and your pension depends on your risk tolerance, you had better be thorough and honest in determining your maximum drawdown. It all depends on *you*. What do *you* want? What are *your* objectives, and *your* risk tolerance? The answers are different for *everybody*.

One of my clients is an ex-floor-trader. He has seventeen years of experience, but he can't trade on the floor anymore because they're closing and shifting to electronic trading. He contacted me in order to create a different approach. We had a long talk about objectives. When he said, "I can handle drawdowns of 25 percent," I asked him, "Are you sure? What is that based on?" He said that it has happened countless times in the past seventeen years. He knew exactly what it feels like, and he was sure he could handle it. I believed him, because he had experience. When a beginner tells me that, I second-guess their estimate immediately. Most people don't know what it's like to lose a quarter of their equity. It's human nature to get upset and react emotionally, and you need to account for that. Failing to do so is the surest path to failure.

People need to accept that they can be smart and make money while also admitting their natural weaknesses.

When I discuss drawdowns with clients, I make them visualize their account balance, to simulate their emotional response. Imagine your initial capital, then imagine the amount you have lost. Let's say it was $500,000, and you said you can handle a 25 percent drawdown. Picture that drawdown of $125,000. That $125,000 is just gone. You look at your account statement every day, and it's not $500,000 anymore; it's $375,000. How do you feel, exactly? How would you feel if eight months later, it's still below $400,000? If you've been trading for eight months, and lost $100,000? Would you feel uncomfortable? Would you still follow your strategy? If you translate the percentage into real money and visualize it, you can have a better view on what percentage drawdowns you can really handle, and how your emotions would change. Nothing is a substitute for real-world experience, but visualization is a good start.

My clients always learn the most important lessons when they lose money, rather than make it, because of our natural bias toward risk aversion. If you're up $50,000, your ego turns on and you tell yourself how great you are. You forget the important things. You don't observe yourself. You just feel great. But when you're losing $50,000, it sticks in your mind. You start to feel anxious and second-guess. You look at your strategy. *Why isn't it making money? Why isn't it doing what it's supposed to?* You start to redefine and reanalyze your objectives. *Were they set correctly?*

You start to feel uncomfortable. Fortunately, that uncomfortable feeling will teach you if your strategy is truly right for you. You only know if you're comfortable trading long and short together—if you're comfortable with trend following or mean reversion—from real-world experience *losing money*. You don't know if a strategy is right for you until you've seen it at its worst and experienced your emotional response. You don't yet know if it's a strategy you can follow for life.

When you're up $50,000, you think about how great you are, and what you're going to buy, and how you're going to retire earlier with more money. You don't analyze your trading; you just pump up your ego.

I can't stress this enough. Your strategy will work and grant you financial freedom *only* if your objectives and beliefs have been clearly defined and tested based on real-world experience. You must know if you will be able to stomach your strategy and still follow instructions when you're experiencing the inevitable, maximum drawdown.

Many people trade stocks because they want fast-paced excitement. Their personality likes excitement, and they think trading is the perfect hobby. This is terribly wrong. If you get excited when your strategy does well, I can guarantee your risk management sucks. Getting too excited about wins means that you are too attached to the money you're making. That means sooner or later you'll be in a drawdown, and you won't be able to handle it.

To be profitable and successful in trading, you need to have a process-oriented approach to trading rather than a results-based approach. That's not exciting. It's quite boring. But good trading is supposed to be boring, because the objective is simply to execute your proven process. You can't look for excitement in the markets; you'll fail. Make your trading boring so you can find excitement in other areas of your life—love, travel, adventure, whatever you enjoy.

Take a long-term view of your trading. Be aware that you will *always* experience drawdowns, even with a proven strategy. In fact, most of the time your strategy will be in a drawdown. The S&P 500 has been in drawdowns for seven years straight, historically. That's way too long, of course. Your strategies, though, will sometimes go through a period of a year or longer where you're not making any money. That's part of trading. In order to make this work, you can't think that time period means anything. It's just like running a business, or investing in real estate. You will have months when your business is losing money, or the housing market isn't good. Trading is the same. You need to look at your results over a ten-year period. What results can you achieve in ten years? It doesn't work if you look at just a couple of months. Trading is not a game where you can make money in a short time. Most who try that go out of business. There might be some lucky people who make a huge amount of money short term, and they'll brag—but they'll blow up eventually, and you'll never hear from them again.

This process-oriented, long-term approach requires you to shut out the noise and go live the life you want. You need to ignore what the media tells you to buy, and what the newspaper says. It won't help you if everyone says gold is going up or down. The only thing that counts is trading your strategy, which follows price action. It's not prediction. The whole noise around investing must be ignored.

A client of mine is a busy executive who has a high-paced job that pays well, and he has significant equity on the side. I did four days of private consulting with him, and we developed a great strategy that consists of several substrategies, well defined according to his beliefs and objectives. He's been trading for seven months and is up about 23 percent, including the big drop in the market in January 2016. He has made over 300,000 USD this year, and is outperforming the index significantly, because he's executing his strategy the way it's supposed to be executed.

He's having such success because he basically acts like a robot now that the work is done. He focuses on his busy job and life. He travels a lot. He schedules thirty minutes a day to blindly enter his trades, and then goes on with his otherwise exciting life. Because of this, January's drawdown had no effect on him, and now he's up big. He understands the value of a robust strategy. This mind-set of understanding that his up-front hard work will gift him a tool he can use for life is unique, and the key to his success.

Because he's so busy, he often does his thirty minutes of trading at 10:00 p.m. We had to make some concessions. We were realistic with what his energy level would be like after work, and so we created a strategy that requires him to enter fewer trades. He wasn't realistically going to put in forty orders at 10:00 p.m., so we sacrificed some potential return. It was better to ensure he would follow the strategy rather than try to maximize profits. He'll still do exceptionally well, and he can be sure he'll follow his strategy.

With your strategy set up to grant you financial freedom, you can start shutting out the annoying noise, so you can live your life. You don't need to look for excitement in the markets, because you can wake up and swim in the ocean, take your kids to school, stay in bed with your wife, go skiing, hiking, skydiving, or do whatever it is that excites *you*. The strategies in this book have been proven, not only based on back testing, but based on the real-world results of my experience and that of my clients.

Now, the strategies in this book are outstanding, but they're not optimized and personalized for *you*. If you're a truly committed trader looking for the best results, visit TradingMasterySchool. com to design your own strategy, step by step. We have various programs—from a video course to my popular, competitive Elite Mentoring program—in which you'll learn together with a group of highly skilled and committed people.

When the back test shows one thing and real-time results show the same thing, that is as scientifically proven as trading can get. This isn't high-frequency trading, with fancy computers that you can't compete with—it's simple, proven trading that has worked for decades, and will continue to do so as long as you do the work I've outlined. Work hard, be honest with yourself, trust your strategy, and enjoy your freedom.

CHAPTER 15

The Next Step

The final step is the most important: You need to *take action*!

The key to success in the markets is to put this information to work, and to *actually apply it to your own trading*, based on your preferences.

The best way to implement what you've learned into your trading so that you can reach the next level—financial freedom—is to join my Trading Mastery School's Elite Mentoring program.

If you *really* want to reach the top, you can join my Trading Mastery School's Elite Mentoring program. Alongside a group of ultra committed traders, you'll build your own suite of non-correlated trading strategies, perfectly suited to your personality, lifestyle, and risk tolerance. We'll take you through everything, step by step, and you'll graduate the program with a perfect strategy you can use for life.

Whether you like day trading, swing trading, trend following, a combination, or anything else, we'll find what's best for *you* and design a solution, together.

You'll have access to our Trading Mastery School Elite software—the same software I use to develop my strategies—exclusively available to Elite Mentoring students.

For more information, visit:
https://tradingmasteryschool.com/elite-mentoring.

About the Author

Laurens Bensdorp is the founder and CEO of Trading Mastery School and TradingSystems.com.

In his younger years, he traveled the world instructing white-water rafting guides—growing their guiding skills and general performance, and developing contingency plans. Laurens's training was highly demanded, and he has worked in Germany, Austria, Turkey, Israel, Dominican Republic, Costa Rica, Argentina, Spain, Brazil, and Chile.

In 1998, Laurens started his own adventure tourism company in Mexico and successfully sold his shares in 2000.

In 2000, Laurens was hired to manage a small boutique venture capital company in the Netherlands. This started his career in finance and helped him discover his real passion—trading and beating the markets. He began managing all of the company's investments, first lowering its risk profile. It was a great learning experience, but Laurens disliked the corporate environment.

From then on, Laurens devoted a large portion of his non-working hours to educating himself about trading and risk management. After years of endless studying, Laurens created a trading style that suited his personality, lifestyle, and beliefs.

He then devoted a decade of his life to developing automated, algorithm-driven trading platforms to maximize profit, while limiting risk, and keeping management time to virtually zero. From 2006 on, he had vast success trading his family's accounts.

Laurens was featured in Van Tharp's book *Trading Beyond the Matrix*, in which he explains how he transformed himself from a losing trader into a winner.

Outside of trading, Laurens enjoys spending time with his family, traveling, wine collecting, skiing, and taking long walks on the beach.

Through his personal foundation, "Fundación Albenco," Laurens and his wife help disadvantaged children in Colombia gain an empowering education.

As a stock trader who only needs his software and an Internet connection, Laurens has the freedom to choose his dream location. Laurens has lived in eleven countries, speaks six languages, and currently lives with his family in southern Spain.

Contact Laurens
Web: TradingMasterySchool.com
Email: info@TradingMasterySchool.com
Twitter: @laurensbensdorp

For blog posts and other free information: TradingSystems.com

Exclusive Offer for Readers

As a thank-you for reading my book, I'd like to offer you *free* access to a video course in which I dive deeper into the settings and parameters of each of the strategies, discussing the charts and statistics in more depth.

Simply visit: *https://tradingmasteryschool.com/book-offer*

Made in United States
North Haven, CT
01 May 2023

36087493R00124